PAIN TURNED INSIDE OUT!
OH, LORD, HELP ME

LINDA GREGORY

Pain Turned Inside Out: Oh, Lord, Help Me!
Copyright © 2018
Linda Gregory

ISBN: 978-0-578-56045-8

Library of Congress – Catalogued in Publication Data

Printed in the United States of America

Publishing Assistance
Jabez Books Writers' Agency
(A Division of Clark's Consultant Group)
www.clarksconsultantgroup.com

Unless otherwise indicated all scriptural quotations are taken from the King James Version of the Bible.

About The Author

Linda Gregory

A graduate of Berkeley College; born and raised in New Jersey, a mother of one, a grandmother of one, and a widow.

I grew up feeling the pain others went through, and from that, I have a desire to help, uplift, encourage, and pray for those struggling with life's challenges. I believe in miracles and blessings no matter how far we fall down, and no matter what our pain or circumstances are. I believe we can get back up through faith knowing we are not alone. Even if you have been betrayed by those closest to you. God is still in the midst.

I'm an ordinary person, not perfect, I have faults like you, but I know God will never leave me nor forsake me. My strength comes from God first, then from my mom and my daughter, they give me strength to help others. Their support through my trials, pain, and tears has been priceless. I want to let you know, you are not alone. Just trust in God and it will get better.

My grandfather's parents were slaves from Buckingham County in Virginia, known as Dillwyn. I enjoyed spending time listening to my grandfather speak about his past; how he worked in the kitchen in the slave house after slavery. How he spoke about the fan in the ceiling, and how he had to fan the people around the table. I could hear and feel the pain of his experience. My family visited the slave house in 2013, and it is still standing. We took a tour through the entire house and property. It is amazing how everything is still intact with the kitchen off from the right where you step down into it where the slaves used to cook. In the back of the house were steps, which led upstairs where the house slaves slept. The log cabins, where the slaves stayed who did not work in the house, are still around the house as well. The house was bought by one of my relatives from the slave master and it was passed down generationally to their family.

When I was 13 years old, my parents divorced. I watched my mom sacrifice and struggle as a single mother. I always felt her pain to see her sad and struggling, but through it all, she kept her smile, her dignity, love and compassion. She went without to make sure we all had everything we needed. She worked on Wall Street with stocks and bonds until she had an accident. She later went back to college to become a teacher and graduated in her 50's. She taught in Newark, New Jersey public schools until she retired. Watching her made me stronger. Through it all, God strengthened her faith to endure.

My prayer is that this book will help you and strengthen you to reach out to the Father who loves you no matter what you've been through, experienced or suffered. He loves you still. May you find a loving relationship with Christ. It is His love and presence in your life that will help you through the most difficult challenges and seasons you will ever face.

Table of Contents

BOOK OF ENCOURAGEMENT   **15**

IN LOVING MEMORY   **19**

DEEP THOUGHTS   **23**

Building Relationships On The Road To Destiny

Destiny

Overcoming Fears On The Road To Destiny

Who Are You Listening To?

Everybody Can't Go With You

God Is Good -- He Is Real

Raising Children At The Round Table

Judge Not

Don't Be Tricked

Don't Let Yourself Down

Success By Design

Can You Hear Me Now?

Raining Inside My Smile

Mothers, It's Not Your Fault

Joy Came After The Pain

With God It's A Done Deal
Battling Depression
How You Treat Others Is A Sign Of Wisdom
Un-Compassionate

SMALL TALK   **51**

Change Your Mind
Who Are You?
Prayer Station
Weeping Won't Last Always
Words Are Invitations
You Are Not Alone
A Good Way To Start Your Day
The Power Of Love And A Sound Mind
Stay Focused On What Really Matters
The Wealth Of Good Health
Be Strong And Courageous And Pray
Helping Family Members Who Discourages You
Created To Be Loved
Equal In His Sight
I'll Pray For You -- Really?
Sleepless Nights
Hearing In The Silence
Easily Offended
Not So Norms Of Motherhood
A Mother's Love For Her Daughter
Encouragement

I Got To Be Alright

Unresolved Pain

Joy

Peace In Your Destiny

The Fruit Of Love

Be Fruitful And Multiply

Family Responsibility

Life Is Like A Puzzle

Generational Curses

DEDICATIONS   97

Dedication to My Mother, Dorothy M. Johnson

Dedication to My Daughter, Salyndria

Dedication to Grandson, Prince-Jalen-Thomas

Dedication to My Sister Sharon

Dedication to My Niece Krystal

Dedication to Four Of My Siblings Who Passed
Away: Horace Jr./Aka Rock/Gary/Jacqueline/Aka
Jackie/Recently Baby Brother, Charles/Aka
Chucky-2017

POETRY   **119**

    Drama – Why?

    A Brother's Anger

    Where's the Peace?

    I Believe

    Are You Confused?

    Deep Thought- Brothers' Uncaring Spirits

    Brother, He's Real

    Don't Take It Personal

    After Thought – Don't Take It Personal

SONGS   **151**

    Power In The Word

    He Gives Me Strength

    I Decree What I Believe

    Thankful Thankful

    My Song To My Grandson

LINDA'S BELIEVE IN SELF, COURAGE and FAITH   **167**
CHART

PRAYERS   **191**

Prayer For Healing and Restoration

Prayer Of Victory

A Prayer Against Depression

My Prayer For You

Prayer Of Expectation

Prayer of Salvation

Book of Encouragement

It is my desire that this book will encourage and uplift everyone who has been through the fire and suffered; was lost spiritually, discouraged and left so mentally exhausted that it affected your well-being. For some, you might have been abandoned in the time of need and betrayed by those you trusted. Some actually thought they had friends that would support them, only to be disappointed when they needed them.

Others might have suffered from lack of employment or lack of experience to succeed in life. While many might have suffered and thought they were not going to make it whether mentally, physically, emotionally, spiritually or financially, but they did. Many had to raise their children as single parents because, in some cases, the fathers or mothers abandoned their responsibilities. I pray that every one of you that have been through the fire and suffered some kind of loss and pain will be renewed in your spirits to know that you are not alone, and God has not forgotten you.

This book has been difficult for me to write because often my pain was turned inside out. I would cry out to God, "Oh, Lord, help me!"

As I was writing this book, my daughter and my first grandson were hospitalized for three weeks with complications. Regardless, I am still trusting God knowing He is Alpha and Omega, the Lily of the Valley, Jehovah-Rapha, Rose of Sharon, King of Kings, the Bright and Morning Star, Judge and Jury, the I AM, and the Encourager. He will always be there when no one else is there. He is there when you think you are alone. He is there when sickness and disease afflict your body and the doctors say, they can't heal you. He is there always. Remember, God will get the glory and you will get the victory.

This period in my life wasn't easy. My pain was watching my love ones suffer. But during this ordeal, I knew who was in charge. This is why this book must be written to let everyone know, no matter what your circumstances or issues are, God's got you. Don't wavier (doubt), God's Word will never return void.

I started writing this book in 2009, without even knowing it; jotting things down along the way from year to year, after experiencing one challenge after another, but still standing on the Word of God. I remembered so many moments of pain in my family, from sicknesses, to untimely deaths, to long-term illnesses. I had to watch those close to me deal with pain and unforeseen circumstances, and we all had to trust God believing things would get better and that we would see the victory in the midst of pain turned inside out.

I watched my mom suffer throughout her entire life with sickness (from her younger years into her elderly years), but one thing I noticed was how she trusted God in all matters. I also witnessed other people's pain turned inside out and watched how they used prayer as a weapon for deliverance. Seeing all of this happen in my family, I realized something about myself, I was a person who could feel other's pain and wanted to encourage them to hold on and don't give up. I wanted everyone to know, they were not forgotten. Regardless, of what we all go through, God is still there to uplift and to sustain us through turbulent times.

In Loving Memory

This book is in loving memory of my sister, Jacqueline/ AKA Jackie; and recently, my baby brother Charles Sr./AKA Chucky (2017); my grandmother Angelina/AKA Angie; my brothers: Horace (Bud/Rock), and Gary; my dad, Horace Sr., my husband, Thomas I. Gregory; and my nephew Gary.

I could not have written this book without mentioning my love ones who were such a part of me. They were my soldiers and I dedicate this book to them. They stood the test. First was my big sister Jacqueline (Jackie). I always admired her and wanted to see just how our lives would turn out. I miss her. She was brave and never allowed her sickness to defeat her in anyway regardless of what she was facing. She was terminally ill and had love to give to her children and family. She never wanted or received pity. She cooked, went to church in her jazzy-style mobile wheelchair, she traveled on buses, and she went shopping. I would joke with her about how I would be afraid the battery on the medical device would run out while traveling. I loved her so much. She was brave and determined. I think of her last birthday celebration, and not knowing it was the last time I would see my sister.

When she passed, I saw the pain on her children's faces, such pain turned inside out. I saw the pain on my mother's face telling her daughter to let go; you have suffered enough. A daughter's pain, the loss of a mother. The son's pain, the loss of a mother. Pain turned inside out.

I think about my older brother Horace (Bud/Rock) who lost his life two months after the family reunion to a heart attack. I felt so bad because I miss him and loved him. He was a kind and compassionate person who never finished speaking to you without telling you that he loved you. He was kind and caring -- loved everyone.

Gary was a brother that stood tall and thin. He was quiet and had a gentle spirit. There were so much joy and laughter when he was around. Boy, did he know how to tell jokes to make us laugh when we were young. He had a unique personality where his presence was known by how he touched your spirit in such a calm way.

He was great in track and in math. I used to watch him pecking on the manual typewriter back in the day before technology took over. It hurt me so bad when he kept having mini strokes. I remember my mom telling the doctors, "No more, he's suffered enough," when they were trying to put tubes down his throat, which was obstructed from the stroke. You could see the tears in his eyes. "No more, no more," she would say. "Stop, my son has suffered enough."

So much pain my mother witnessed from her children. When I have flashbacks, it brings tears to my eyes. Even while writing this, my eyes are tearing.

My nephew, Gary, who I called little Gary, grew up to be a handsome young man with so much love, and a sweet and quiet like spirit like his dad. He was a wonderful person. I remember asking him to go to church with me just before the family reunion, and he said yes. I told him, "When you come back from the family reunion, we will go," but that never happened because he drowned the last day of the family reunion. Pain again, just pain. For everyone, especially his mother and siblings. It was a shock to all who loved him so much. I loved him very much as well. I pray the Lord will continue healing my entire family.

In addition to all this, I had to take care of my dad, who suffered with emphysema, for ten years. When he passed, it was a nightmare. I remember after he passed, not hearing the noise from his oxygen machine in the house, and how the house was quiet -- no more talks and laughter. I traveled up and down the highways for ten years caring for my father while there was another loved one battling cancer, my husband, who was undergoing chemotherapy. I also remember those drives to Deborah's hospital outside of Fort Dix in New Jersey.

There was so much pain, grief, and sickness that plagued our family that I became numb, but I kept on praying. God kept me strong in all my pain.

I have learned to never put things off for tomorrow because tomorrow may never come. If you have never been through so much pain from losses, it is hard to imagine. Love your family while you have the chance, call them often, drop by often, get together at family functions, so you will never have regrets because of difference of opinions and stupidity. When they are gone, they are gone, and they are gone forever. The pain will linger in your heart and spirit, but through God's love you will be healed.

DEEP THOUGHTS

I used to think if you missed your time or wasted it, you lost your opportunity. However, after listening to a sermon by Bishop T. D. Jakes on "Finding Your Gifts and Talents," something interesting resonated in my spirit that I began to think about how many of us never talked or had conversations with our parents about their gifts and talents. It caught my attention because I knew my mom had many talents and gifts, but I never discussed them with her. I just knew she could do a lot of things. Bishop Jakes stated, "You, too, can have the same gifts and talents as your parents, but you don't know it because you never talked about your shared interests and experiences." It really "hit" me when he said, "Do not allow your parents to be buried with their gifts and talents without finding out if you have the same gifts and talents within you. Who knows, some might be a business."

Later in the week, I mentioned to my mother that I wanted to purchase a bracelet. To my surprise, she said, "I can make that for you." I was shocked. She laughed and stated, "You kids never listen to me when I tell you what I have and can still do at my age." She had been doing handcraft for over 30 or 40 years. This reminded me of what Bishop Jakes said in his sermon. From that moment on, my mother and I started making Christian bracelets. Even at the age of 87, suffering from arthritis and other medical challenges, my mother is sharing her gifts and passions with me, and I am happy to be learning from her. Working together led to many other shared interests such as aqua exercises, computer classes, and of course, cooking.

I have learned not to allow disappointments or sickness to stop me from fulfilling what God has ordained for me. He is the only One I know who can heal, deliver and open doors that are closed. I am blessed to be my mother's caregiver.

Building Relationships on the Road to Destiny
We are all different, and we all think differently, so you must not look at someone else's life and compare it to yours. Everyone is on his or her own level. Your successes will be at your level. Do not get disappointed when your success is not moving as fast as you would like. Sometimes God keeps you at a certain level in life until you have mastered it and learned the lessons necessary to move forward. These can be lessons of faith, belief, patience, respect, humility, compassion or just trusting in Him. Before you reach your destiny, you must know how to handle it. You must know how to treat others with respect and dignity, including your loved ones and close acquaintances (your family, friends, and co-workers).

God gives all of us talents and gifts, but we all, at times, are challenged with some level of fear that can cripple our progress and prevent us from realizing our destiny. To overcome these fears, we can pray and listen to what God is saying regarding these times. This will often mean putting yourself in a place where you can hear God's still, small voice in prayer or when reading His Word. If you can't find work, ask yourself, "What can I do with the gifts and talents I have?" Take the time to talk to your parents and grandparents; you might discover a great idea that can lead to a million-dollar business. This is just a thought.

Overcoming Fear on the Road of Destiny
Sometimes when you are going through your trials, you may not have anyone in your "corner." In times like these, you have to encourage yourself just as David did (1 Samuel 30:6). Through your tears and pain, you must depend on God's strength more to get you through life's challenges knowing He is the only way. When we put our total trust in Him and stop taking it back through worry, frustration, and anger, He will see you through all your adversities.

It is hard not knowing how life will turn out. Trust me; I've been there many times. I know what it is like to be completely stressed out and crying but still praying. I would pray through my agony with faith believing God to heal my loved ones and strengthen me along the way to my destiny.

God is greater than doctors. In fact, He is the One who instructs them. Times will come when they reach their capacity in the medical field; they don't have any cure for our illnesses. We must put all our trust in Him. He is the Lord of lords and King of kings. He is the Prince of Peace when you can't find peace. His peace surpasses all understanding. He is the Alpha and the Omega (the Beginning and End). He knows everything we are going through even before it happens. He is our Advocate. He is Shalom, the Rose of Sharon and the Judge. He is the only One who can judge you. So stop worrying about what people say about you because it does not matter; they are not God.

People who talk about you wouldn't do so if they had a flashback of their own lives. Actually, they wouldn't speak negatively about you or anyone else. No one is perfect on this earth. We have all sinned. Therefore, do not let what others say about you cause you to be fearful or stop you from doing what God has purposed for your life and destiny.

Fear paralyzes us. It will stop you from thinking straight, concentrating, and moving forward in life. Fear can also hinder our relationships and opportunities. It can prevent you from using your gifts and talents by highlighting your weaknesses and what you can't do. Hence, you will focus on that instead of trying to do what God said you can.

Who Are You Listening To?

The problem is that sometimes we listen to the wrong voices. I have learned that the voices of fear are there to distract us from where God is leading us. Fear tries to confuse us, so we won't know the difference between God's voice and that of the enemy. You must know God's voice. He will not send you in the wrong direction. He will not give you the wrong advice, but He also will never override our free-will choices. It is up to us to decide who we will listen to: people who are negative, small-minded, self-centered, dysfunctional, and "jacked up" or that sweet, soft voice of God who is all-knowing waiting for you to hear Him. His Word of Truth can change your situation, uplift, and encourage you, as well as put you on the road to having a stable mind and spirit.

Trust Him. He loves you and wants to see you do well. He wants you to be proud of your accomplishments. He wants to unify and stabilize your family. He wants you to have a good job and take care of your family. He wants you to use your gifts and talents. He wants the best for you and your children. God doesn't want a generation lost in the streets with no respect for self, authority or parenting. The bottom line is He has a plan for each and every one of us. But it is our choices that will set or determine our destination in life.

When you don't listen to what God is saying to you, you will be led in the wrong direction. When you allow people to mislead you and never think for yourself, you will always be a follower instead of a leader. You have to stop, think, be calm and listen to your spirit to hear God's Word speaking to you. God speaks from His Spirit to your spirit, but you must know His voice. Otherwise, Satan will put doubt and fear into your mind, which is not led by God. The negative images you see in your mind are from the Devil, not God. God doesn't give you false images to sway you to think or do wrong. We all have free wills to make our own choices. God will give you signs to let you know you are headed in the wrong direction before it is too late.

Be careful who you listen to. If it doesn't sound true, it probably isn't true. Negative people will fall easier because they're not anchored in the Word of God. You don't have to be a fanatic to listen to the positive Spirit of God and what He is trying to say to you because He will never lead you wrong. He orders your steps into all truth. If you pray, listen to what the Spirit is saying. Then receive the word for your life and make a plan for success. You will be successful! For God knows the thoughts He thinks towards you – thoughts of peace and not evil, for an expected end. God expects your end to be successful (Jeremiah 29:11).

When I was going through many trials and witnessing the suffering of my family members, I would repeat this to myself throughout the day, "God wants me and my family to be healed." He wants happiness for all. He knows the suffering we endure, but His joy will come in the morning. What we are going through is only temporary. After the suffering (the rain, tears, sickness, and deaths), God is still there. He will never leave you alone. In due season, you will rise again. Don't give up! It might be painful. You may have setbacks. You might be misjudged and treated badly. Nevertheless, God is still in the midst of it all to deliver you. He heard your cry. In my distress, He heard my cry, and He helped me (Psalm 120). Get your strength back and get back up. He loves you; trust Him.

Everybody Can't Go
It can be painful to some or relief to others, but everyone can't go with you when God is shifting you in life. Let's face it; everyone is not in God's plan for your life. Everyone doesn't have what it takes to go with you where God has ordained as your destiny. You see, He will remove people from your life, especially dysfunctional people who have no business being a part of your purpose and destiny.

You may need a smaller circle of friends in your life, instead of a large group of friends. Often, in this season of your life when God is shifting you, having too many friends can cause confusion, dysfunction, and jealousy. Everyone is not your friend. Someone very special to my heart once said to me, "Put up your hands and look at your fingers." I did. Then he said, "Show me two fingers." And I did. After that, his words spoke to me in a way I will never forget. I passed these words down to my child. They are from my daughter's dad and my husband, Thomas I. Gregory, R.I.P. He said, "These two fingers represent your friends, the rest are associates. If you find two friends in a lifetime, you have found your friends. The rest are people who pretend to be your friends (fake friends; friends with agendas)."

Your true friends stand with you in times of trouble when others are nowhere to be found. True friends will be honest and have your back. They won't talk about you or discuss your business with others.

Be careful who you tell your business to and who you listen to. Don't be a follower just to be in the crowd. It means nothing if you're not where you ought to be in life. Normally, these people you are compromising for have nothing to offer you. Connect yourself with people doing great things and going somewhere in life. Also, make sure they are godly with a servant's heart, compassionate, humble, kind, loving, as well as caring with a great spirit. The fruit of the Spirit will show if it's in their hearts, spirits, and minds. In addition, check out their intentions. A friend whom I loved very much once said to me, "You have a beautiful spirit." She was a wise, beautiful, elderly person inside and out. She also said, "I can tell a person by their spirit and if their spirit isn't right, neither are they. Just check out their spirit, it will tell you a lot" (Ms. Daisy Stevenson, R.I.P).

The Lord is my strength and shield my heart trusted in him and I'm helped therefore my heart greatly rejoiced and with my song will I praise him (Psalm 28:7).

God Is Good - He Is Real

When trouble comes, life is stressful, and you have no one to trust, know the Lord is your strength and shield. He will protect you from unseen dangers and pain if you trust in Him. Also, it is important to know, we are never completely shielded from everything. However, He will lead us out of the darkness into the light. All things work together for your good when you put your faith and trust in Him. Through it all when you look at the goodness of Christ, you will know He is good, and He is real.

Raising Children at the Roundtable

We must raise our babies in the Word of God because the Enemy is out to destroy them. If we don't, we will have a lost generation.

It pains me when I look at the younger generation because they are lost and do not know it. Many of them have no respect for themselves, their parents or anyone else. Every day, they are losing their lives in the streets due to violent crimes, gangs, and other negative behaviors. It is very sad. Even our schools have become unsafe with fighting and bullying. What has happened to our children?

I believe they are lost because God and prayer are no longer in our schools, homes or parents. Therefore, godly living is not in the children. Parents must be anchored in the Word of God to learn how to raise their children. Having a sound knowledge of the Word of God will help you when you need to discipline your kids. It is impossible to teach what you don't know yourself.

When I was a child, if I didn't go to school and church I could not go outside to play with my friends, no exceptions. The only reason we didn't go to church or school was because of sickness. Period.

We all must do a better job of protecting our children from bad influences. Please, don't lose your children to the streets. How can you do that?

*Pay attention to your children
*Form a meaningful relationship with them
*Communicate to stay connected with their lives
*Start a roundtable with your children, so you can hear what's going on with them

My mom would sit us down and we would discuss what was on our minds. We resolved the issues we had among ourselves. When there were problems, we would find common ground so we could end disputes. My mom called this our "Roundtable." I pray for unity for families, and that they will have peace and love from within.

Judge Not

Please, don't become narrow-minded after God lifts you up and changes your life. Always seek to help others. Be a blessing to someone else and share your story to assist others. As you become blessed, be a blessing, not a curse. Too many Christians forget where they started out and how God turned their lives around.

When God blesses our lives, this is not a time for us to look down on others. God looks at the hearts of people, not titles or who we have become. Christians must make others feel welcome, have a servant's heart and not be judgmental.

Help others rather than judge them. You never know whose life you will save by caring and taking notice instead of gossiping about the person who just may need a caring ear that day. Your support, love, and compassion will encourage more people who are struggling and hurting to seek God, the healer of our souls. That way, they can become who God called them to be. God commands us to love one another. He didn't say judge one another. Sure, I know everyone with a ministry title is not called of God. It is true that even ministers can be judgmental and negative at times; therefore, they cannot help the hurting.

How can people who are judgmental ever recognize those who are hurting? Too many are committing suicide because they feel they can't talk to anyone. I have seen that pain. I remember going to the funeral of a child under the age of 12 years old who committed suicide. I also had a close friend of my family, whom everyone loved, jump off the eighth floor of a building. We were all shocked. He always looked sad. I would ask him from time to time if he was okay, and he would say yes. I felt bad because there were signs of depression, but he never revealed his pain to me. If you are struggling with depression, you don't have to take your life; there is help for you. Please let someone know, for this, too, shall pass.

Suicide is not what God has ordained for you. Whatever you are going through is temporary. It just seems like forever when you're going through it. Talk to someone if you're depressed, frustrated or angry all the time. Your loved one will suffer if you are not around.

Please reach out, even if the challenges you face involve your loved ones. Call a helpline – 411. Talk to someone. Please, don't take your life. The spirit of defeat is not of God.

As Christians, we must make a greater effort to reach the hurting. This involves praying, helping, and interceding for others. Let's provide an avenue whereby those who are hurting will feel welcome to come to us for help.

In this country, we must learn how to accept our differences: colors, races, religions, genders, and lifestyles. A person's lifestyle shouldn't matter even if you disagree. We must stop hating. Only God can judge. Hence, we ought to pray for people; not despise or talk down to them. People will be more receptive to what God has to say if we share it out of love and not a judgmental spirit. Love is powerfully positive when expressed.

People whose lives have changed for the better should cease from criticizing others. Destructive criticism has a negative impact on many people's lives; it causes depression. With constant criticism, many believe there isn't anyone to discuss their problems with or pray with during the times of need.

The Devil is a liar. There is hope and help. The people who are supposed to be serving God or be Christlike must get back to what God says – to help, sacrifice, pray, and save souls. Your calling is to save lives, not complain about their complaining. Sometimes you need to know the difference because everyone isn't complaining. This is just their way of crying out for help. And if you miss it, you will lose another to the streets, suicide or depression.

Don't be Tricked

Satan is the enemy of God. He will do anything to convince you God is not real. The fact is Satan is a liar. He is the father of all lies. At times, you will feel defeated, and it may seem as if nothing will get better; this is the trick of the enemy to get you to believe his lies. But hold on to God's unchanging Word. Even in your darkest hour, don't let go. God has all the power in His hands. Read and study His Word; it will bless your life because God is real.

Don't Let Yourself Down

When you trust in God, He will work it out for you. Your faith and belief in His Word will bring about His will for you. However, when you try to fix your issues yourself, not having faith in His Word, doing it with a carnal mind and your own strength, you will fail. It will lead to undue stress, disappointments, frustration, anger, and sometimes feeling worthless. It will get worse until you humble yourself and give it over to God by faith. Even if it is a mustard seed of faith, He can still intervene on your behalf. Trust Him even when you can't see any results.

God is the Alpha and Omega (the Beginning and End) of all things. He knows your heart and how much you can handle. He wants you to know what you are made of. He doesn't want you to crumble. He will put you into the fire, so you will know what you are made of. He has given you strength, but you must discover it and know you can do all things through Christ who strengthens you. God made you strong with wisdom and knowledge. Whatever you need just ask and you will receive. He has provided all you will need in this life.

Suffering is a part of life. It is how we grow and depend on God, not ourselves or others. Man can't help you. You may disappoint yourself but God will not. He is all-knowing.

> *The God who called you into eternal life, after you have suffered a while, he will remold you and make you stronger and firmer (I Peter 5:10).*

> *For He knows the thoughts He thinks towards you, thoughts of peace and not evil for and expected end (Jeremiah 29:11).*

Success by Design

God's expectations are for you to succeed in all things. He never wants evil to fall upon you. On the other hand, the enemy's design is to keep you stressed, crazy, dysfunctional, in despair, lost, confused, and a failure in life. He uses fear to control your mind and paralyze you. Hence, you can do nothing in life, and you will accept things that are wrong for you. The enemy will choke you with guilt, so wake up and smell the coffee. Get out of that depressed and confused state of mind; get back into the fight. If you don't quit, you will win.

Can You Hear Me Now?

Are you comfortable with yourself? If not, why not? In order to move forward in life, you have to know and be comfortable with who God made you to be. As stated earlier, some people listen to others who give wrong, negative, and ungodly advice. Don't do that. Make sure you receive advice from godly people who have your best interest at heart. If not, you are going to find yourself living an alternative lifestyle that God did not plan for you.

There is a saying, "Never allow others to create your world because they will always create it too small." When you receive advice from the wrong people, this is the world they are creating for you. Sure enough, this is a distraction from the Devil who came to get you off track in your walk with God.

If you are listening to the wrong people, you will not hear God clearly, especially about those He has not ordained to be in your life. Furthermore, if you continue like this, you will lose out on your purpose and destiny or, at least, you will suffer delays. Remove yourself from negative people and those who do not have your best interest at heart, no matter who they are.

Raining Inside My Smile

Tests and trials often come at inconvenient times when you might have so much more already going on. All of a sudden, another "bombshell" explodes, which leaves you wondering why now? How will you ever be able to manage the new unexpected circumstances and issues piled up on top of what you are already dealing with?

At times like these, you wonder where is God? Why must I go through this? Don't I have enough pain turned inside out in my life already? With tears running down your face, you cry out within, "Lord, help me. I can't do it without your help. I can't figure out why this is happening. The stress is too much. I'm a good person. I love the Lord. I go to church. I pray every day. I'm good to people. I treat them with kindness. I'm respectful of others. I have a good heart and a great spirit. I care about others. Why am I always going through so much pain? Why must I cry all the time inside? No one sees my pain."

People walk around with smiles on their faces; yet, they are suffering inside. Wow! It is unbelievable how many people suffer in silence and feel they have no one to talk to because of the fear of being judged. Their pain is turned inside out and if God doesn't fix it, it won't get fixed.

Many people today are lost and suffering. Therefore, we need to look at hurting people differently. Stop thinking everyone is simply complaining because for many, this is the only way to communicate the pain. If someone is crying out over and over with the same concerns about himself or loved ones, please don't ignore the person's concerns. Pray for him.

This is for mothers who have lost a child through violence or sickness. Most mothers do the best they can with what they have to raise their children. Mothers have so much love for their children. So, mothers, do not blame your-selves for what happened to your children. It was out of your hands. Evil took over and they fell into the hands of the wrong people or sickness and disease took over their bodies – still not your fault. In life, some things are just out of our control.

Some things are ordained by God, while others are attacks from the adversary who came to steal, kill, and destroy our families. He is a liar. It wasn't your fault that some people were not raised to respect the lives of others. One child's bad home life could lead to the loss of your child. Unfortunately, if someone pulls out a gun or does acts of evil intentionally to harm another person, he or she should be held accountable for those actions. God did not do this. Everyone has a free will.

The wicked and the evildoers are at large waiting to take over our children. This is why we must stay prayed up, so we can fight the enemy with the Word of God. The Word of God is mightier than Satan's actions.

Whatever the reason joy was stolen from your heart, whether your children were harmed or you lost the love of your life through sickness, please, know someone cares and is praying for your healing. Today, I pray for your restoration. I pray God strengthens and gives you joy for your ashes. I pray God ministers to you, so you can get back up and keep going. I pray that the memories of your loved ones bring you comfort knowing their spirits are still around watching over you.

Mothers, It's Not Your Fault
May the memories of your loved ones turn your pain into laughter and smiles just thinking about them. May the love you shared encourage you to get back in the race. My mother lost four children to sickness. Some of the losses were sudden, while others were from sicknesses that lasted a long time. Often, I prayed for her. She always said

when she lost her children, "It was like losing a part of her." You don't know what it is like to lose a child unless you have experienced it. Whether it was through violence or sickness, a loss is a loss. Mothers, you are loved. Neither you nor your children are forgotten.

I ask the question all the time, "Why God? Why do people suffer from childhood to adulthood? They see so much suffering and not enough relief, while others walk around without a care in the world. Why my child? Why so much adversity, pain, frustration, anger, and hurt?" Over the years, the stress and hurt flooded my life as I watched my siblings and mother in so much pain. At times, I could not bear it, so I had to turn it over to God to get the answers and the relief I needed.

Joy Came after the Pain
The death of my four siblings still pains me today. I had to deal with the pain of not having them around in my later years. I always wonder what we would look like aging. I don't have answers, but I do know God will help ease the pain of loss. He will help your heart heal. He will restore you after the storm. May you receive peace knowing someone cares about what you're going through and the pain you have endured. Also, I pray that in time, God will restore you and give you your joy back through His love. Lord, help us in these difficult times. Only You can touch and restore.

With God, It Is a Done Deal

Have you ever suffered from an illness such as high blood pressure or any other chronic condition and nothing the doctors did seemed to work? Yet, the doctors kept increasing your medicine until there was nothing else to try, then the waiting game began. When you come face-to-face with this reality, remember, God is still able to deliver. Adding God and His power into the mix, you will see Him always do what the doctors and medicine could not. We must trust God's Word. He will never leave you or forsake you. He is mightier than the doctors and medicine. His Word says you are healed by faith, which is the substance of things hoped for and the evidence of things unseen. "Without faith, it is impossible to please God. For whosoever cometh to God must first believe that He exist and that he rewards those who seek Him in truth" (Hebrew 11:6). God is able. Today, take a chance on His Word.

Battling Depression

When people think of depression, they often think about someone who is sad or whose life is spiraling out of control. There are many reasons someone might fall into a depressed state. It could be because of negative events that may have happened in their lives: sickness, disease, the death of a loved one, disappointments, life-changing experiences, frustrations, recurring events or abusive relationships (mentally or physically). Any of these happenings can be overwhelming and cause someone to enter a state of depression.

Depression can also be triggered by the unhappiness of giving too much of yourself and receiving little back. Mental and physical abuse, heartbreak, loneliness, and rejection can also drain a person emotionally and spiritually causing depression.

If you let them, the images in your mind will take you deeper into depression, which can lead to health issues. Seek help right away to come out of depression, so you can be healed and take your life back. It is the job of Satan to take your mind and put you in "a place of no return," but God came to give you abundant life.

Coming out of depression often takes time. Help is out there. Talk to a friend, a counselor or call 411 if it gets out of control. If you are feeling depressed, you are not alone. Everyone may experience some form of depression at some point in his/her life. However, choose not to stay there; fight to get help. Depression is a serious illness that must not be ignored. It has caused many to take their lives because they were hopeless and felt there was no help for them; this is not true. Connect with a church and get involved. Rise up, get up and take your life back!

When we think positive and receive God into our spirits, minds, and hearts, we can conquer the enemy. The moment adversity comes in our lives, we can reach for the Word of God that will give us strength through our darkest hours. The Lord will walk with you, and you will get the victory.

Friends and family members; know the signs of depression. This is essential. If your loved ones are upbeat one minute and sad the next or they stop talking (withdrawn, stay in bed, stop socializing, constantly crying, etc.), these are red flags that something is wrong. Don't ignore them. The enemy is planting seeds of fear and hopelessness in the lives of your loved ones to steal and destroy them. Satan has taken control of their minds and is telling them their lives will never get better; this is how they will be forever. These are lies from Satan. You have to know that most of the things he projects in your mind or the minds of your loved ones are lies from hell designed to keep you depressed, so you can miss out on God's blessings.

How You Treat Others Is a Sign of Wisdom
God gave you a family; how do you treat them – with love or hate? Do you respect them? Do you have compassion for them? Or are you hateful, mean, acting ugly, and full of the anger and frustration you had before they came into your lives? How do you act toward employees? Do you use or abuse your title and authority? Abuse comes in all forms (mental and physical). Are you mean and hateful toward them?

I have witnessed people who were abusive to the spouses God gave them. It was like a nightmare. You are better than this. So many people don't give the people God brought into their lives a chance, not understanding they are missing out on blessings. When you do this, eventually, God will allow these people to be removed from your life. You took advantage of their kindness, quietness, love, humility, compassion and now they are gone. Be careful how you treat those God gives you, especially your wife. He says when you find a good woman, you find a wife.

Too many people do not take God's Word seriously until it's too late. Also, be careful not to take advantage of friends that God place in your life. God surrounds you with certain people for reasons: some to learn from, others to help push you into your destiny, and some to assist you in changing how you view other people.

Uncompassionate

There are times when women wonder why men are so uncompassionate, frustrated, and angry on the inside. Some are argumentative and have uncaring spirits. If this continues, it will affect their lifestyles and relationships – families, marriages, and friendships. Unfortunately, if children are involved, this can affect them as well, even to the point of passing down generational curses from spirit to spirit, mind to mind, and heart to heart. The same uncaring ways and attitudes with no love to give will pass down into the family line.

A lot of this has to do with fatherless homes and (parents) even though most men would not admit it. The father plays a major role in the family. When there is a void there, it affects the entire household. Sadly, the child grows into an adult and reacts negatively because of the missing element – a father in the home.

I remember when my mom divorced. I was 13. It was very difficult for me. My mom became a single parent who did the best she knew how under such circumstances, but it severely affected my siblings and me, especially the males. I saw so much pain in my baby brother's eyes because he missed his father. Let's be clear: it does not matter what age this occurs. That missing link will affect you as you grow into adulthood.

The wives, who had no idea what was ahead of them until they said, "I do," suffer immensely. Usually, they do not see the truth about their spouses until after the marriage. The missing father leaves voids in the lives of the significant other or spouse, the children, and in the home. Divorce and separation damage the family structure. The divorce rate is on the rise in many cases because men and women carry the baggage of the past, which has not been dealt with into their current marriages. They never got healed from their past hurts and disappointments, which led to anger, and bitterness. These days, men are so sensitive, you can't say anything without their feelings being hurt because they were hurt from the void or abuse from the past. Hurt people hurt other people.

I pray that a revival will take place in all men who were missing their fathers due to circumstances beyond their control that left them hurting on the inside. They lack love from their fathers. May God touch every hurting spot in their minds, bodies, spirits, and hearts. May their souls be revived. May they take control of their emotions again and have the calmness and peace that surpasses all understanding.

If you are one of these men, God has not forgotten you. He knows you did not have the relationship with your father you needed. God knew it before it happened. Please do not get angry with God. He gives us all choices to make but unfortunately, those men made their choices – or the choice was made for them. Perhaps there was incompatibility or other family issues (cheating, lying, and abuse).

Whatever the reason you are fatherless, just know you have a Father in heaven who loves you so much. He wants you to be renewed in your mind, spirit, and heart. He wants you to take control of your household and be the man and father God intended you to be. He wants you to know how to love your wife and children, so the family can grow together with the love of Christ in their hearts. He already told you to love your wives as Christ loves the church. If you don't go to church and have a prayer life with your spouse and children, then how can you be who God said you ought to be? He already gave you instructions on what to do and how to treat your family in His Word.

Never take your family for granted. Rather, allow them to help you heal by whatever means it takes (counseling in the church or counseling from a professional). Get the help, so you do not repeat your father's mistakes and bring generational curses on your family. Start fresh!

I encountered several males who are harboring bitterness but cannot see their problem. Actually, they do not want to see that it is a problem on the inside that reflects pain, hurt, disappointments, betrayals, and unkept promises from their fathers. Many are missing in action. Some dads are taking care of children who are not theirs in another household. That is great but do not forget your own children. This is a priority. Even if you are not with the mother, you still have responsibilities to your biological children. At the end of the day, the children are suffering from the lack of attention from their fathers. You may be supporting them financially but spending quality time with them is equally important to these little ones.

I missed that growing up. It's important not just for your sons, but for your daughters. They choose their significant others based on the type of dad they have. If they don't have an example of how a man is supposed to treat and respect them, some might fall prey to the type of man you have become. A look-alike with no responsibilities, who treats her any old way because he believes that's love. Life will be a nightmare for your beautiful princesses – your daughters.

"Step up to the plate," fathers. Save your family before you have regrets in your old age. You may need them to hand you a glass of water one day. You will get old one day. Secure your place with your children the right way. I'm no expert, but experience and what I witness every day have taught me plenty.

We do have a lot of good fathers who have taken on their responsibilities and have become who God said they are. They love their children and wives as God said they ought to...the way Christ loves the church. These men are passing down love, kindness, humility, compassion, prayers, faith, and belief in the Word of God. They have put God in the center of their lives and families as the third cord to guide their paths to their purpose and destiny. I salute you, fathers, who did not allow your past to cripple your future and the destiny for your life and family.

SMALL TALK

Change Your Mind

Never bring an old mindset into a new year if you expect great, new accomplishments and blessings in your life. If you don't change the way you think and operate, nothing will change. You can't put new wine in an old wine bottle (Matthew 9:17). You can't take your old mindset into a new location or relationship and expect a different outcome. It won't work. We must learn to balance our lives with our family, children, and work. With all the demands on your time, you may say, it's unrealistic to expect you to strike a balance. But it is possible. Actually, it can be as simple as how you think and prioritize the activities in your life. Family comes first with God as the head and in the midst.

Who Are You?

You have to know who you are and who you trust. This means you must know your purpose, values, priorities, and who you are in God. God will not put anything on you that you cannot handle or get the victory over. He made you strong; you just don't realize how strong you are. Yes, our strength is tested through the fire, but the fire makes us stronger and wiser.

Prayer Station

We must learn to stay prayed up all the time. It is important to have a "prayer station" in your house where you can go to communicate with the Lord. Prayer is important even if you don't see a change right away. Prayer strengthens you daily and keeps you focused on your vision and dreams, as well as God's purpose for your life. Prayer anchors you in the Word of God.

I always wanted a "prayer kneeler" for my prayer room. One day, I was very happy to run across Pastor Archie Saul who has been blessed with a vision and talent to make prayer kneelers. He made me my very own to use in my private prayer time as I seek God. It is Pastor Saul's vision to put prayer back into homes and get us on our knees. I am quite passionate about this project and would also like to bless people with prayer kneelers.

Weeping Won't Last

Sometimes when you are the one going through difficult times, it is hard to believe everything is going to be alright. But life's tests come to make you stronger. They help you to trust in God, even when you can't see your way out of your mess.

You may believe God for healing but don't see it immediately. Nevertheless, don't give up. Keep believing. God will never fail or leave you. Yes, I admit it is hard when you are in pain and cannot find relief or a voice to encourage you. Yes, I know what it is like to cry yourself to sleep. I know what it is like to wonder if things will ever change. I know what it is like to suffer; yet, continue to pray and believe in God's Word. Yes, it is hard when your faith is being tried in the fire, but you must believe.

God knows the thoughts He thinks towards you. He loves you unconditionally. Stay in your prayer room until victory comes and never abandon God's Word. You must continue to stand. When you are strong in the Word, the enemy will have an impossible task of taking you down. When he can't do that, he will try to go after your children and other loved ones. Hence, you must keep them covered in prayer also.

Words Are Invitations
When I think of spiritual warfare, I think of a fight in the spirit and mind. So many people believe the battle we fight is in the natural because they witness things happening in the natural, but it's deeper than that. It's darkness from the spirit of Satan, not from God.

Sometimes we battle within ourselves. I believe it stems from the way we think, speak, and view who we are. Living negatively opens your life to darkness. We are warned that Satan roams the earth seeking whom he can destroy

(1 Peter 5:8). He preys on our weaknesses, low-self-es-teem, frustration, anger, bad experiences, and childhood tragedies. Your reactions, the negative words you speak, how you treat yourself and others open the door for Satan to launch his attacks. And he will.

A loveless childhood can be the reason for bad relationships in adulthood. Satan knows if you were abused. He takes all of the things that make you feel inadequate and uses them against you. He will try to make you become who you were never intended to be.

Be careful about how you view yourself and others. Be wary of the words you speak to and about yourself. What you say has immense power to attract good or evil and to determine outcomes. Unfortunately, many of us never realize how powerful our words are. They will produce positive or negative results. Therefore, you should speak only positive words about your children, family, and you.

You Are Not Alone
Grief can be completely overwhelming, so in times of sorrow when you are all alone please, trust in God. He knows everything you're going through. He understands the pain of loss and is walking with you even though it seems as if you are alone. He is with you through the storms, in your weakest hour and times of need. God is holding you up; that's why you're still standing.

Sometimes you might not realize it is God who is sustaining you, but trust me; He is a very present help in the times of trouble. Only God can carry you. After losing her four children, my mother once said, "I thought I would go before my kids. It's an emptiness that you just can't explain because it is so painful." She always said, "I feel as if a part of me is missing."

My siblings were very special to me. Being raised together, we shared so many things and wonderful moments. We all had different personalities. Now, the laughter we shared is gone forever.

I've witnessed so many losses in my family. I have seen some of my loved ones take their last breath. The pain and missing them is real, but in the shadows of grief and in spite of the agony, I learned to trust God.

A Good Way to Start Your Day
Knowing that tests and trials, sickness and suffering are a part of life, we have to make a decision every day to stay positive. Betrayal, feeling defeated, and depression come at some point in our lives, but don't stay in despair. Don't let your emotions eat at your core when God is trying to bless you. God can't get to you because of the choices you have made and the wrong voices you're listening to; yet, He waits for you. He is rooting for you! He wants to walk with you through all your issues. Depend totally on Him.

He will save and deliver you completely. Why not start to-day by giving your life to Christ? He loves you so much He wants to see you set free.

Stay Focused on What Really Matters

What are you looking at? Have you ever wondered why other people seem so happy, but you are not? Why do others seem so successful when you are not? Why do others find happiness, while you can't, even though it seems you are doing all the right things in search of love, happiness, and success?

It could be that the enemy wants you to look at others instead of focusing on you and what God has for you. You can never tap into your God-given potential, vision, purpose, and destiny if you keep comparing yourself with others and agonizing about what you have found. What God has for you is for you. The enemy knows if you've changed your thought life and renew your mind (asking God for wisdom and knowledge), he has no power over you.

You see, if the enemy has your mind, he has you totally. Break free of the old you and renew your mind to release the person God has ordained you to be. When you do this, strongholds of the mind will be destroyed; unbelief will fall; lies will go; strength will be renewed, and Satan will have to flee. The Word of God is powerful all by itself.

So, keep your eyes on what really matters. I would be lying if I told you it's going to be easy because it's not. It takes commitment and strength to stay focused. As I was writing, I had to jump up because of excruciating pain in the muscles of my feet and legs. But I told the Devil I am determined to write this book to encourage others regardless of my pain. Fibromyalgia or osteoporosis won't stop me! I remained focused and continued writing. The passion in my heart cries out all the time, "Oh, Lord, help me to be able to help others."

I thank God for His Word that is being poured into my spirit from my (Pastor) Bishop T. D. Jakes. I just don't go to church for a performance. I go to be healed spiritually, emotionally, mentally, and financially, as well as to pass along generational blessings. I want to leave a legacy for my daughter, grandson, future not yet seen great grandchildren and generations to come. At any age, you can do anything through the power of God's Word. It's never too late and you are never too young.

The Wealth of Good Health

One thing I have learned in life is without good health, money means nothing. You can live in a fine mansion, but if you cannot get up to get a glass of water or dress yourself, money means absolutely nothing. I always tell my mom and my daughter nothing matters without your health. All the money in the world means nothing without your health. Yes, God promises wealth, but please pray for good health over wealth. The rest will surely come when you act on God's Word. He is real. His creations are real. He truly heals, delivers and sets those in captivity free. Pass your test and go to your next level of life.

Be Strong and Courageous. Pray
What do you do when your children/parents/loved ones are going through life's trials, and you're trying to be strong for them? What do you do when you have to witness the suffering of your children, parents or your loved ones dealing with sickness and pain, and there is nothing you can do about it but pray? Alone, you cry because they are suffering, and you can't do anything about it but cry. I experienced this pain watching the suffering of my child, mother, father, husband, and siblings. I witnessed it over and over again in my family.

It took love, strength, tenacity, and dedication to be there for them with encouragement and prayer. We prayed together and separately calling on the name of Jesus Christ. I have cried out to Him many times, "Jesus, Jesus, Jesus – I need you now. Please send your angels and cover my loved ones." I know when we call on Jesus, mountains move. When we put our faith together an explosion of miracles happen and blessings come down from above. The doctors don't have the power of Christ. They can only do what their training and capacity allow them to do. What do you do when they have reached their limits and you are not healed? You must reach out to a higher power – have faith in Jesus Christ.

The power of God through Jesus Christ can set you free through the power of His healing Word. "If my people who are called by my name would humble themselves and pray, and turn from their wicked ways then will I hear from heaven and forgive their sins and heal their land" (2 Chronicles 7:14). Your faith in God's Word will heal you. Rely on His report and His Word to heal your spirit. Keep praying no matter what the doctor's report says or what you have to go through.

God will also heal our land. Are you in the land? When we call on God's name in prayer, He shows up in hospitals throughout the land. He shows up in nursing homes, families, and minds. He makes crooked places straight in our land and lives. Father, I know You are a healer. I pray that revival takes place in our homes, hospitals, and jobs. I pray that people will create healing environments in their spirits trusting in the Lord.

Helping Family Members Who Discourage You

Have you ever tried to help family members, but it was like fighting a battle by yourself with no returns? It's very disheartening and discouraging, and it can drain the life out of you. Sometimes it leaves you feeling unappreciated and disrespected. To top it off, they think you're supposed to help them because you have been doing it for so long. They have become totally dependent on you.

Maybe you are mentally exhausted; your strength is depleted, and it seems as though no one cares. Ask yourself if the love you have for your family members is stronger than the love you have for yourself. Have you forgotten to prioritize your life or are you letting others prioritize it for you? Do you think God directed you to kill yourself over people who don't value you or what you do for them? The answer is no. And it is time for you to "wake up and smell the coffee."

God didn't tell you to drain your life for them. God didn't tell you to lose yourself in them. God didn't tell you to keep helping people who don't appreciate the fact that He put you in their lives as a divine helper. He did not put you there to be abused physically, emotionally, spiritually or financially.

God didn't say take over their lives. He said give them help. Don't get lost in their world thinking your only purpose in life is to serve them. I learned a valuable lesson about this – to listen to what God is saying to me while I care for others. You see, God wants to teach us how to help others – how much time to give and when to let people take responsibility for themselves.

I know what it is to be a caregiver. As a young woman, I spent 10 years caring for my father around the clock. He was on oxygen 24/7, and I traveled up and down the highways caring for him, even though I had to work late hours at night. I know firsthand what it is like to care for loved ones like this. It can be overwhelming. At times, you feel as if you have no more energy left to give. I'm used to multi-tasking, but that, too, can drain you if you are not careful.

I also know what it is like to be a caregiver to more than one person at a time while having to work and take care of a child. My daughter would always tell me, "All I ever see you do is take care of people and work. You need to slow down and take care of yourself, so you can be around for me and my generation to come." She is right. Listen to your body before it is too late. Caregivers need someone to take care of them, too.

It can be such an honor to care for loved ones who appreciate what you do for them. Right now, I have the privilege of caring for my aging mother. She has given me more love than I could ever repay. My life has been enriched as a result of caring for her. I now have an opportunity to reciprocate some of the love she has given me over the years.

Created for Purpose

I woke up one day, looked up to the heavens and saw sunshine and blue skies. I said to myself, "For God is the Creator of all things. He gives us sunny days, cloudy days, and rainy days. Wow! God is so real!" The sky, moon, stars, and planets wouldn't be here if it wasn't for our Creator, God. He gives us darkness at night and light in the day.

When you know God is real, you understand the sun, moon, and stars are not just sitting there for us to observe. They are there for a reason just as we are. We were created in God's image for a reason and a purpose. Some of us just haven't realized our reason or purpose, but God gives us clues along the way through life experiences. It is imperative we all find the reason God created us. God loved us so much He made us in His image so we can receive abundant life and the love He gives freely.

Equal in His Sight

When I look at our society, I see many people who are sad. I also see those who are wicked, full of hatred, and prejudice. I often wonder why? I wonder why one race thinks it is superior or better than another when the Bible clearly states God created us all. He created the earth for all of us to live together, not separately. Together, we share God's creation. We enjoy the sun, which gives us light during the day; the moon, which gives us light during the night. The stars, the planets, they all show the beauty of God's creation. He made water and air to breathe available to all. He created us to live together as one and to be fruitful. So why does a group of people or race believe God's creation is just for them? I am confused.

This planet and its resources are meant for everyone, not one group or race of people. It is time to stop racism, hatred, and prejudice in this country and all around the world. If we are one, we are equal. Therefore, we should all have equal access to shelter, food to sustain us, and opportunities for employment. There must be equality for all races and genders.

Equally concerning is the hatred I see within all races and communities, even where low income families reside. People hate and hurt their own. This also needs to stop. It just makes no sense if you are trying to raise good families and succeed in life.

Some people have no value for life, theirs or anyone else's. Why is this? Spiritual apathy and moral decadence. Prayer and family values must return to our homes, schools, and communities. Without God in the center of all things, our societies will become more violent and divided. People say, "I believe in God," but they neither act as if God exists nor do they practice His unconditional love. We must do better.

"I'll Pray For You" – Really?

I often wonder when people say sometimes, "I'll pray for you" – REALLY? Or are they just saying it to get you out of the way? I wonder how many people really keep their word. How can we expect miracles and answers from God if we don't pray? Lazy people can't hear from God. He can't answer what you don't pray for or present to Him. Prayers are an important part of our lives if we want answers. Sometimes it may not be the answer you are looking for, but it is God's answer to you for that season in your life. Prayer gives strength, wisdom, and knowledge to those who ask. It renews our minds and helps us to forgive. Forgiveness is necessary for healing and deliverance from the people who hurt, wronged or betrayed us. We have to move on.

Forgiveness does not exempt the person who wronged you. It is for you to get healed, so you can leave the past behind and move forward to receive what God has for you in your life. New vision, miracles, blessings, relief, destiny, and God's purpose for you are just some of them. Enjoy what God has waiting ahead for you. Don't be like Lot's wife in the Bible who turned into a pillar of salt because she looked back when the Lord told her not to.

Your past is your past. If you don't let it go, it will always haunt you, and you will stay stuck where you are with no growth. If you don't renew your mind daily, how can you think beyond your circumstances? You cannot overcome the trials you are facing with a negative environment and mind. If you don't let these negative thoughts go, you will be like an idle car, stalled in one place, not moving. God wants more for you and your life, as well as the people He has connected you with. Through prayer, you can release many bad memories that haunt you throughout your life. In fact, they were never designed to be in your life in the first place. Cancel the nightmare of a stuck mind, then move on and get what God has for you.

Dream big. Expect bigger. You can receive it with God through the power of prayer. Connect with someone who will pray with you when you are not capable of praying for yourself. When two or three come together in God's name, mountains can be moved. Obstacles that were stuck will move. People who impeded your progress in life must move out of your way.

Sleepless Nights
At night when you're going through trials, and you don't know what to do, just fall on your knees (if you are able) and pray to God for relief. You may have to sing yourself to sleep. You may have to pace the floor at night and pray until you feel a release. Regardless, just know – you are not alone. You may not talk about those harrowing nights when you walked in fear of the unknown or those days you worried about what God said He had already done, but even in those times you were not alone. Sure, you

had no tangible evidence that God had already done what He said He would, so naturally, you were on edge as you waited. So much so you wondered what you were thinking about or praying for.

In weary nights like this, I have found myself singing, "Oh, Lord, tell me in the night what I must do to hear Your voice whisper in my spirit what my purpose is." In the night I sing. In the night I pray. "Oh, Lord, what must I do to release all the anointing You put inside of me? Oh, Lord, what must I do? I'm ready for Your wisdom. I'm ready for Your love to hold me so I can feel secure. Oh, Lord, what must I do? Oh, Lord, I thank You for answering me. I thank You for giving me the peace that surpasses all understanding, so I may rest at night without fear, worry, and the imaginations the enemy is trying to put in my mind. I know You are able, and I thank You for what You have done in the past. By saying that, Lord, if You did it for me then, I know You won't disappoint me now even if it looks like nothing will change. I trust You."

When thou lieth down thou shall not fear.
When thou lie down thy sleep shall be sweet
(Proverbs 3:24).

We all have sleepless nights, twisting and turning, walking the floor, fearful of what we think may happen, or what is yet to come. We wrestle with thoughts Satan puts into our minds to make us think God's promises won't come to pass. We get sidetracked because of these things we often cannot talk about, which create stress. Some people even lose their minds and become very fearful. God did not give us a spirit of fear, but power, love and a sound mind (2 Timothy 1:7). Again, we have power over the negative images Satan uses to confuse our minds to keep us from believing in God and that we have the victory.

Also, when we are under attack and can't see our way clearly because the load is too heavy, we need more than a mustard seed of faith. It's a lonely road when you feel you are in it by yourself, and you cannot talk to anyone. It can be very scary, but this is the time we need to pray even harder. Cry if you must, but don't stop praying until your breakthrough comes. Victory is yours. Our hearts may be heavy at times and the trials and tribulations may seem too hard to bear, but the majority of what you think are lies straight from the pit of hell to try to get you to deny God. He is real, and He answers prayers. He may not come when you think, but God is always right on time.

Prayer for Sleepless Nights

My prayer is that your heaviness be lifted and that you feel relief. I pray God touches all the hurting areas in your life and renews your mind.

Father, touch them; give them a new beginning with a renewed spirit. Let the bondages of Satan be broken off every mind and erroneous mindset. Those who have had sleepless nights not knowing if victory will come, not knowing if healing will come, not knowing if life will get better, not knowing if their loved ones will get better or come back, not knowing if their kids will change for the better and not knowing if the streets will take their kids, let them have peace today, right now.

Father, I ask for a hedge of protection to be around the minds of Your people. Give them hope. Give them victory. Give them healing in their finances. Give them hope for their children. Give them hope for their marriages. Give them hope in their pregnancies. Give them healing in their hearts, minds, and spirits. Don't let the enemy have his way in their lives in any way. You said they can have life and have it more abundantly. You said to multiply. Father, I pray for peace for everyone who needs You to come into their lives and give hope, healing, and victory in all things (Proverbs 3:24). You said when they lay down, they shall not be afraid, and their sleep shall be sweet.

For He knows the thought He has towards you. Thoughts of peace and not evil for an expecting end. He expects you to have sleep and peace. He's got this; quiet your mind, spirit and rest (Jeremiah 29:11).

Hearing in the Silence

Silence doesn't always mean to shut up or be quiet. It could mean quietening your spirit, so you can hear from God. Get in a quiet place and pray or read the Bible, then let the answers you need flow from your spirit. God speaks to us through our spirits. Being quiet (hearing from God) can be your answer to what you need. Sometimes by just reading the Word of God, you may hear God's answer to your prayer. If you have too many things going on in your head and you are distracted by too many voices in your mind, how can you truly hear from God? You have to get alone and be silent sometimes.

Father, today I pray for every distraction and voice that is not of You to be shut down right now, so Your people can hear Your silent voice in the spirit giving them the answers they need to change their lives and circumstances. I pray for broken hearts to be healed. I pray for dysfunctional thoughts to vacate their minds and spirits. I pray that their emotions will be healed so their souls may be healed. May

69

they return to the Word of God if they have left, so they can get back on the right track. Let every silent prayer be answered.

May the love of God return to each and everyone who wants to let go of distractions, dysfunctions, anger, frustration, and hatred that have been lingering in their spirits because of past hurts. May all be healed, delivered, and set free from emotional bondages that have kept them locked up in their minds – physical and spiritual damages from people and the drama in their lives. Let it end today so their silent prayers can be answered and that they may be healed for You to do new things in their lives. May they be anchored around truly caring people who will hold them accountable for their actions so they can stay on a straight path called happiness and joy. May they have the peace only You can give.

Love yourself and pray for your haters. Learn the gift of "goodbye" when you have had enough with the drama. It does not matter if it is your family, job, friends, acquaintances or associates, trust God even in your silence. He will never leave you or forsake you. He hears all of your prayers even when they are unspoken. Keep praying and lifting those prayers up to God. He will answer in His own way.

Easily Offended

People who get offended easily are difficult to understand because they are always living through their feelings. It is sad because they cannot find their greatest potential when they are easily offended. When you become upset over nothing or something so minor, you allow others to control you technically.

Those who are quick to take offense distort the truth and become the victims over and over again. Then you end up taking the high road to explain how you didn't mean to offend them. I have met many people who are always offended; it is like talking to a brick wall. They hear themselves but nothing you are saying in a conversation. I find them to be sensitive and always finding fault of other people; they never look at themselves. Whatever you say or do is a problem with them. It is not right or up to the standard they think something should be.

Most people don't like drama, so they tend to shy away from people who are always offended. The truth is it is mentally draining when you always have to try to explain a situation or action they have distorted in their minds. God does not want any of His people to feel offended, hurt or not loved because of the lies the enemy has projected in their minds and spirits. God understands how you feel. He understands the pain you feel from what you believe to be true, but it can be distorted at times. God wants you to be healed emotionally, spiritually, and mentally. He wants

71

you to know that sometimes it is your perception that is distorted because it is not always true. God does not want you to worry about things that are taken out of context, which lead you to act a certain way. Don't be judgmental over foolish remarks that are not going to further your career, life, family or household.

Sometimes people can say hurtful things because they lack the ability to reason. But you cannot take every word to heart and get offended. God loves you, and He wants you not to be so sensitive that people's words dictate your actions or your words lead to drama.

Lord, may this word touch those who always feels offended. May You touch minds and heal Your people who have been hurt by offenses and bad attitudes. Bless them in a mighty way. Restore their minds and spirits, so they will not listen to negative voices that lead to complaining spirits. Amen.

The Not So Norms of Motherhood

This is a touchy subject because of the pain I suffered as a result of a miscarriage years ago. When I hear people say, "Just get over it," it makes me want to scream. Some believe there is no pain from a miscarriage. Are you kidding? Being in the hospital in the maternity ward hearing other people's babies cry when your room is silent is heart-breaking, to say the least. The pain, discouragement, disappointment, and emotional stress can be unbearable. I don't want to hear another man say, "Get over it." This is why you need a great man who understands, has compassion, and can empathize with your pain and loss. Maybe it is easy to say, "Just get over it" because they don't see the baby. This is cold and heartless.

There are mothers who went through the entire pregnancy, then lost the baby full term. These women suffer tremendous pain. It is heart-wrenching coming home empty handed without their bundle of joy. Instead of welcoming pure joy, they have to prepare for a funeral. Mothers who have miscarriages after going full term often fall into depression. This is when they need you to understand their pain the most. Whatever a woman is going through during her pregnancy, she needs a compassionate, understanding man by her side. She needs a man who will understand her ups and downs, that some days she may not feel good and doesn't want to be bothered. Other days she may not feel like eating everything and will be very picky.

Some women deal with sickness through their entire pregnancy, so it is important to have that caring man by your side who will stand with you during your bad days, as well as your good days. You need that support mentally, emotionally, physically, and financially. As a pregnant woman, you need to feed your spirit with the Word of God, so it can empower you to overcome the challenges in your life.

Motherhood is underrated and taken for granted because women have been giving birth since the beginning of time. People look at it as a norm, especially men. They don't think about what a woman goes through just being pregnant. Her body is changing; her moods are shifting, and her mental health is often stressed. Most men never think of it as a full-time job when a mother is juggling her schedule even after birth and dealing emotionally with the changes in her life.

It's even more frustrating and painful for single mothers who have to do Mommy and Daddy duties all by themselves. My heart goes out to these women because I know the struggles my mom had to deal with in parenting after her divorce and raising her children by herself. But she did it. I love her for raising seven children alone. To all the single mothers, may God bless you double for the trials and tribulations you had to endure with little or no help.

I just have to pause for a moment to thank my grandma Angie for being the best grandma ever. She "stepped up to the plate" to help out in all areas when there wasn't anyone else to do so. I will forever love you from heaven. You were the best grandma, full of love to give. She became a mother to the disabled children where she worked until age 86. She always said she had a direct line to Jesus and no one had to pray for her. She could pray for herself. She loved all of us. I salute you, Grandma Angie Strickland. You are missed dearly.

I spoke about the silent prayers previously, but I want to touch on the silent prayers of women who want to have children of their own. However, circumstances or health issues are keeping them from becoming pregnant.

I pray for you who have placed that request before God and are still waiting. May miracles take place in your lives. I pray that God blesses your womb to be fruitful and to make a liar out of Satan and the doctor's report. May the crooked places be made straight. May you become pregnant miraculously. I pray that you and your baby will be healthy and protected throughout your pregnancy. May a reverse of what is keeping you from becoming pregnant be far from the truth. May God's Word become the light in your life. I pray you will have the right significant other/spouse to be at your side (God's selection for you), so the blessings of generations will be upon your children. Amen.

A Mother's Love for Her Daughter
There is no greater love than the love of God. The love of a mother toward a daughter is a special bond that is often beyond understanding. It is a love that is so dear and close you can feel her pain, sadness, and frustration. You know through her eyes without her saying a word that she is going through trials. You know what her smiles and her missing smiles tell you. They can tell you when she is happy and sad. It is exciting when you know she has

found happiness in all areas of her life. But also, when the excitement has gone from her eyes, you will know the difference. You feel the void and pain that she feels without anything being said. It's unspoken. It's like God knowing when you are sad or happy; when you are going through or in the valley of darkness. He is all-knowing.

Your mother's love helped (created) you and gave birth to you; therefore, she knows your pain, character, attitudes, love, happiness, disappointments, and frustrations. A mother has a powerful connection with her daughter. Not saying she doesn't have it with her son (because she has a special bond with all of her children and loves them unconditionally), but she has that special relationship with her daughter. I'm just speaking about a mother's love for her daughter.

You really can't fool too many mothers and if you do, for some reason, sooner or later the truth will be revealed about everything to her spirit without a spoken word. She knows from expressions that something is wrong. She may not know all the details, but one thing she does know is something is definitely wrong or bothering her daughter that she may not want to talk about. She may not be able to put her "fingers on it," but her spirit signals a problem. She knows, so open up and let her in. She may have gone through the same thing you're dealing with. Talk to your mother because her love and understanding are amazingly strong. If you are one of those special daughters who have or had a strong relationship with your mother, be thankful.

I dedicate this to all the mothers who understand exactly what I'm talking about and have that special bond with and love for their daughter(s). God gave that special gift to all mothers who accept it. Never take advantage and dismiss what God has given you: a chance to love His gifts of life unconditionally as He loves you. He nurtures and guides us, and then lets us go into the world to make choices. The same as your mother does. She protects, nurtures, loves, guides, and then lets you go into the world to find yourself, to follow your dreams and visions, as well as your purpose for your destiny. Some will go off to college; some will move out to be on their own, and others will get married. No matter where they go, a mother's love will stay connected. Her heart will still feel her daughter's pain, happiness, sadness, joy, and disappointments. No matter what age, a mother's love is unconditional.

Like everyone mothers do have faults. No one is perfect even with their love. Motherhood didn't come with a book, so it's a trial and error position. Mothers have weaknesses and strengths just like everyone else. When things happen, children can suffer from the lack of motherhood. Know that some mothers aren't always the mothering type. It may be because of what they went through in life and how they were raised, so they have no reference to go by to raise you. This is why we need to be understanding, and perhaps, try to find out why and what happened that left them clueless about motherhood. But the most important thing is that we don't become angry and repeat the cycle.

A person cannot give you what they never had or was never given from their own parents. But we do know that if they have God in their life, they can find the love that they need to help give you what you need -- unconditional love of a mother.

When you raise the child up right with God in the right environment, she or he will blossom into that person that God ordained with wisdom, knowledge, love, compassion, humility, kindness and affection. Some people don't know how to love or give affection because they never witness it in the house between their parents or in their family, but God gives all the love you will need to love Him, self and others. Love is powerful, and we must put it back into our homes, families, marriages, and with our children, so they can grow up with the love of God, and in return, they will give good, honest, and pure love that is by the power of God.

Encouragement
Have you ever cried out for help and it seems as if no one was there? You felt as if everything was crashing down on you and you couldn't find relief anywhere or any kind of encouragement to uplift your spirit. It's a terrible feeling to feel alone and you can't find anyone to help. You may need

guidance, but it seems as though no one is listening. This is when you find yourself all alone and it seems like you are carrying the weight of the world on your shoulder.

You have to encourage yourself when you can't find a soul who cares what you're going through. They don't understand that you are being emotionally, spiritually, physically, mentally or financially challenged at this time in your life. You just need a fresh word to get you through these obstacles. The Word says, if two or three of you, touching and agreeing on earth; asking anything of the Father in heaven, He will answer you and you will receive what you are asking for. However, if you don't have anyone to come into agreement with you, then this can be challenging. But you still have to know God hears your cry, and He said in Psalm 120, "In my distress I cried out and he heard me and helped me." You still have access without the two or three, just know that He gave you the power to change your circumstances through His Word even when you can't find encouragement or someone speaking into your life. Speak and encourage yourself.

God has already given you motivation, determination, drive, encouragement, and the peace that surpasses all understanding. Don't allow people to stop you from encouraging yourself when no one hears or answers you. People have to learn to hear what God is saying. If you are doing God's work, then do not push people away from you that are crying out for help. We all go through sometimes whether we admit it or not. No one escapes suffering.

Prayer of Encouragement

May God touch His people that were called to be His servants and flush out the fake servants who thrive on titles everywhere in the church, in homes and on jobs. Bless Your people, God, so we all can see newness and unconditional love You given freely. May God strip all the judgmental spirits and complaining attitudes and bring peace to the Body of Christ so Your people will be healed. For You said in Your Word: "If my people who are called by my name, shall humble themselves, and pray, and seek my face, and turn from their wicked ways; then will I hear from heaven and forgive their sin, and heal their land," (2 Chronicles 7:14). Father, we need healing in the church; healing in homes; healing in the workforce; healing in marriages; healing in families; and healing in our children. Please heal, set free and help Your hurting people, and allow Your servants of God to be humble and have a compassionate spirit to pray for the people who need them in their darkest season. Amen!

I Got To Be Alright

In January 2012, this saying kept playing in my head, "It's got to be alright, Lord." I just kept saying to myself, "It's got to be alright, Lord. Lord, it's got to be alright. Because we are standing on your Word. It's got to be alright, Lord. It's got to be alright. It's got to be alright, Lord. It's got to be alright. Cause we are standing on your Word. When the fiery trials come, Lord, we're standing on your Word, Lord. We're standing on your Word. When the fiery trials come, Lord. You said it's going to be alright, Lord. You said, it's going to be alright, Lord. It's going to be alright. We're standing on your Word, Lord. We're standing on your Word, Lord, because you said, it's going to be alright. Lord, when the adversary says, "We look like a fool standing on Your Word and saying it's not going to be alright." So we lift up our hands and pray more to You, oh, Lord. Because we're standing on your Word, Lord. Why do we suffer, Lord? Why do we suffer? But we know that no matter what, we are standing on Your Word, Lord. We're standing on Your Word, and it's going to be alright."

"Lord, why do we suffer as a child of God? But we're standing on your Word because everything is going to be alright. Everything is going to be alright. Everything is going to be alright, because the Bible tells us so. We're standing on Your Word. Everything is going to be alright, everything is going to be alright. Everything is going to be alright."

When you and your family is going through, you have to come together as one standing together on one accord; on

81

God's Word. I remember just saying, "No matter what, we're standing on Your Word, Lord. It's going to be alright because we're standing on Your Word." Trials and tribulations may come, but you have to know that only the Word will bring you victory. When sickness gets out of control and surgery is pending, I have learned in tears to gather the family together, in-person, and on the phone to pray. This is what I do when there is a need in my family. Even when I can't get to the conference call, I ask everyone to please pray for one another and please, if you can, put everyone that's going through on the prayer list at your church. One thing I can say regardless of all the different religious backgrounds in my family, we still manage to put all that behind us and pray for one another. I'm grateful to have a praying family in all religions. We never judge each other when it comes to prayer. We come together as one for victory on one accord.

Unresolved Pain
Adversity, confusion, dysfunction, frustration, anger, lack of humility, no compassion -- when I look at these words, I see negativity. I see lost souls. I see hurting people. I see adults who grew up with unresolved childhood pain. Pain that carried into their adult relationships (marriages, family life, and with their children). This is so sad.

These unresolved issues affect everything they do and the people they associate with. I would like for them to know that prayer and getting in the Word of God will help them overcome these issues. Therapy is sometimes needed and should be used in dealing with some of these deep-rooted issues. Too many people are walking around holding hurt, grudges, pain, unforgiveness, and wondering why they're stuck in life; not realizing that they have to let go of the past. When God removes you from the past, you are not to go back to those dead issues.

God cannot take you where you don't want to go. And you can't hear Him with so much dysfunction going on. Satan comes to kill and steal. If you remain in the past and refuse to let go, you will become dysfunctional, frustrated and anger will continue.

Forgive and stop tormenting your soul with what you cannot fix by yourself. You need God in the midst of all your situations, circumstances and past pain. Regardless whether it is from your childhood or past relationships, you have to stop hurting yourself with images of your past. You're missing out on happiness, joy, and peace in your spirit if you don't. Love is the greatest and you are missing out on your blessings by drowning in your pain and self-pity. You have to learn to turn your negativity into a positive with the help of God.

Let Him heal your past hurts. Why lose out on all your dreams, visions and the purpose God has for your life. God loves you and He doesn't want you to continue hurting and living in anger and frustration. God knows your pain and He is the only One who can turn your life around. Step up and let it go. Love is better than hatred. You are better than sadness. You can be healed and set free from the entanglement of Satan's web if you let these things go. If Satan has your mind, he got you totally, along with your peace, joy and happiness. This issue is so important because so many people are walking around in silent pain ready to explode from the inside.

Joy

Joy is better than happiness because happiness can be temporary, but joy comes from the inside, no matter what is going on in your life. In good times and in bad times the joy of the Lord will be in you. Even in your sadness, the joy of the Lord will be there. I used to say, "Where is my joy," but as I got older, I realized my joy come from the Lord, which is not based on feelings or circumstances, but based on the knowledge of the Word of God? You may be sad, upset or don't even feel happy, but if you are one of those people who still read God's Word, still prays and goes to church in spite of how you are feeling, you got joy. Just stay with God, He loves you so much, and He doesn't want you to suffer but He knows suffering is a part of life even though we would like to think it isn't. He is ever-present, so reach back and grab that piece of joy you thought you lost. Joy does come in the morning even though sometimes it can take weeks or months. He got you, don't give up on yourself.

Peace in Your Destiny

God gives us peace that surpasses all understanding. Sometimes we get so caught up in life situations and worldly things that negativity causes us to lose our peace not even realizing when and how we lost it. All you know is that you feel like you have no more peace. We forget the peace that God gives us when we turn to Him, and put aside worldly things (and negativity), which in most cases are the reasons why you lost your peace in the first place. Also, being caught up in "he says, she says or they say" are peace stealers as well. You give every inch of your peace away to someone else worrying so much about things that doesn't matter; things that are insignificant. Walking in peace on a daily basis is almost abnormal. There are so many things that can cause you to get frustrated and agitated daily, and if you are not careful, you will become the negative "thing" in other people's lives stealing your own joy and peace away from you. You got to fight for your peace every day. You see, God wants us to walk in peace every day, but Satan wants us to walk in fear and frustration. This is why he fights so hard in our imaginations to create negative situations to disrupt our peace. But let me say this also, sometimes God will position you to be agitated by people "to get on your nerve" to push you to a higher level of maturity. This is why you need to have a close relationship with God, so you can discern the difference. As well, you need to surround yourself with people who are going somewhere. Sometimes agitation can push you into your destiny. It's God's will for you to be blessed.

The Fruit of Love

Being fruitful is not about money. It is about being fruitful in all aspects of your life: your personal and family life, on your job, etc. That which God has called us into, we have to be fruitful. Some people automatically think being fruitful is about money. If you are fruitful only in your finances, then what about your health. Would you rather have money or your health? Would you rather have a mansion and can't get up to get yourself a glass of water? You need to be fruitful in all areas of your life. Health is the number one priority of being fruitful.

Also, you want to be fruitful in your mind because the enemy can come and steal it. Mental illness is a very serious problem in our society, so you want to have a "rich" mind. When you are fruitful in all aspects of your life, don't complain about what you do not have.

Lord, I pray for the people who have been praying for the fruit of love. Open their eyes to the love You have provided. The devil is a liar. God is still in charge and He knows your heart and knows what you need. Reach out to Him so He can heal you, so you can be fruitful in all areas of your life. God is love.

Be Fruitful and Multiply

Whatever God gives you, He wants it to multiply in the womb of your spirit. When you produce what God has given you, it will be greater than what you started with. The enemy wants to multiply fear in your life. But God wants to set you free from fear and fill you with faith. You must learn to trust God enough to allow Him to come and "plow up" your life. He may need to root out closet skeletons and replace them with a new attitude.

Satan has assigned fear to block up your womb and cause you to be less productive than God wants you to be. Don't be afraid. You are God's woman/man/ no matter the desire or the blessing that you seek. God has promised to give you the desires of your heart (Psalm 37:4), and He will always keep His promises.

Family Responsibility

Are we really responsible or do we just talk it? When it's time to be responsible, do we show up? Some people always have excuses about being responsible. Will they be responsible as a husband or wife? Are the children responsible or have they become too lax like their parents? When kids show signs of lacking discipline and no responsibilities, what do you do? We all need to be responsible and have balance in our lives. Parents have to take back their responsibility in the home and stop giving it to the children to do whatever they want. No structure in the household, then we wonder what happened to the family. The responsibility left when the fathers left the homes, dysfunction creeped in and no one ever noticed it until it was too late. Fathers need to become responsible again, so children will know what responsibility means.

LIFE is like a Puzzle .

Life is like a puzzle. Trying to fit the pieces together day by day to match the parts of the puzzle. Where do you start? How do you finish? The puzzle can be complicated if you don't know God's purpose and vision for your life. Just trying to fit in everywhere will not work. Sometimes you might feel lost and out of place. Life can be very hard at times when you're confused and lost.

It can be especially difficult when seeking wisdom and direction, but He will give it to you. He will lead and guide you into all truth. As you continue to walk in Him, He will give you testimonies to the glory of God. Sometimes you may get off track and get lost, but through His Word and help from the Holy Spirit will assist you in getting back on track. God orchestrates all the pieces together (all things work together for the good to them that love the Lord and are called according to His purpose). The grace of God who called you into eternal life, after suffering for a little while, will renew you and make you stronger and firmer. He already knows where the puzzle of your life fits. He's walking with you, and as you walk with Him, the pieces are being put back together through your faith and prayers. "Trust in the Lord with all thy heart and lead not unto thy own understanding." Keep walking the puzzle out until all the pieces fit and it's a finish product of God.

Generational Curses

Generational curses are a part of every family alive upon the face of the earth. For my family, as stated earlier, sicknesses, diseases and tragic deaths are the generational curses we have had to endure. These negative traits and habits have been passed down from one generation to another, and yet, people haven't figured out where they come from. I sometimes wonder why? Why have my family suffered so much pain and unbelief? If it isn't this happenIng; It's that. If a person is suffering from one thing, then this same thing will be passed down to another and on to future generations.

I have been praying most of my life to break the generational curses in my family. I watched my dad suffer from emphysema and lung disease, hoping that God would heal him only to watch my elder sister suffer from emphysema and lung disease also (they were both on oxygen), which they eventually went on to be with the Lord. Then later on my mom ended up on oxygen. She never smoked. Often she would have spasms that would impair her breathing ability. She suffered the same way.

In addition, my baby brother suffered the same way for a while on oxygen. It was really painful for me to watch all of this. I had to stop and ask the Lord, "What's going on? You said we can have what we speak out of our mouth. Your Word said whatever we bind on earth shall be bound in heaven and whatsoever we loosed on earth shall be loosed in heaven (Matt 18-18)." Then I would speak this in the atmosphere, "Father, You said if we trust You and have the faith of the mustard seed and speak Your Words, it shall come to pass."

But yet, it kept happening. More sickness, from stents in the heart to high blood pressure to congested heart failure. But I never stop praying. In fact, I will never give up. You see, I know now, it is about setting the next generation free from these generational curses in family.

When I pray, I pray generationally – for now and for our generations to be born. I want my family lineage to be healthy. We have to start the children early on taking care of their health. Yes, I know somethings are out of our control, but I am still bothered by them. I just want to see my family healed and these generational curses broken off their lives forever. I know I am only one person, but sometimes it just takes one person to break generational curses in your family, regardless what they are.

Each family upon the earth are plagued with different generational curses. These curses can be sin passed down, and you have nothing to do with it. They could be from your parents, grandparents, or great-great grandparents' sin; things you might not know. Believe it or not, but it could be something passed down from ten generations? Your family can be constantly dealing with stuff and you are wondering where did this come from?

Over the years, I have found myself thinking about this. I have sought God about this throughout my life in Christ. I asked God not to let any of my sins (knowingly or unknowingly) to touch my children and children's children, and so forth. I would also pray the same thing regarding my parents, grandparents and their parents' sin, that they would not to be passed down to the next generation. I would pray and ask God to go back 10 to 25 generations, if possible, to cancel out anything anyone ever done (knowingly or unknowingly), so that my generation from my mother to her children, and children's children even to her fifth generation be protected under God's generational blessings.

It didn't matter if it was sickness, unemployment, or lack of. Whether it was mental health, finances, smoking, drugs, or fibromyalgia. Whether it was lying, cheating, depression, anxiety, heart disease, lung disease, diabetes, heart attacks, cancer, strokes, blood diseases or liver disease. I would call it out by name. These diseases and negative traits have all been passed down in my family from somewhere, and probably yours, too, if you have similar issues. Ask yourself is anyone else in your family going through the same thing that another family member has or is going through. If the answer is yes, this is what is called generational curses, negative traits or diseases passed down from one generation to another or another person in the same family lineage.

This does not mean, it is your fault by any mean. My mom did not ask for heart disease and congested heart failure, and she surely did not ask for her son to die from a heart attack that shocked everyone, but it happened sadly. Personally, I am tired of seeing my family suffer. I want these generational curses canceled in my family. I am so sick of losing siblings through sickness. I am tired of seeing loses in my family and lack of from struggling to succeed only to get depressed. Whatever happened in November 2010, was a clear indication that I must not stop praying to God for cancellation of generational curses in my family.

On the other hand, we must start speaking about generational blessings. The blessings of Abraham which you are connected to if you know Christ. I don't know how many people think or know about generational curses, but I know for some, they do not believe it. I know bad things sometimes happen to good and faithful people, but we still need to cover our families according to the Word of God. If you see consistent bad things happening in your family, you owe it to yourself to at least pray for generational curses to be broken in your family lineage.

A lot of things I will admit is from what children see and experience in their household like violence and crime; but these things still can be broken off the next generation. It can be simple things like smoking. Smoking can be a generational curse. The father smoked and ended up with emphysema, now his son or daughter is experiencing the same thing. Dad or mom got a lying spirit, now the children has the same spirit. This is how generational curses are identified and passed on, so it takes someone strong in their faith to break them.

Your dad may have been on drugs and his dad or mother may have been on drugs, so you have to take authority over it and say, "This is where it stops. The 'bucks stop here.' I want my life different. I want to see and experience the generational blessings not the curses." It can be just a choice to change the way your life and your family life live to a new normal of blessings instead of curses.

Prayer To Break Generational Curses

My prayer is for families generationally today that they may think differently regarding their families and their future. The unborn to the young, and to the old that we may began to see light instead of darkness, pain and tears. I pray now to break the strongholds off of your love ones and their entire family. I thank You, Lord, for breaking strongholds not just for three generations, but 10 to 20 generations.

I pray especially for our youth and teenagers that suicide and bullying be cancelled out right now. I pray for a revival to hit these young people and that their lives will never be the same. Thank You, Christ Jesus, for dying on the cross to protect generations. Oh, Father, even if the children and family members don't understand what is really going on, I truly pray for wisdom and understanding generationally, so they may take note of what is going on in their families. I pray that strongholds and their love ones that are bound be loosed today.

Father, I thank You for cancelling out pride, perversion, depression, frustration, crookedness, disrespectfulness, disbelief, fear, anxiety, foolishness, fear of failure, high minded, ignorance of the Word, and the lack of self-control.

Now, Lord, I thank You for bringing back to all generations the blessings of the Word. I release every generational blessing that has been held up because of sin and generational curses. I command them to be loosed right now and to flow freely throughout the generations to come. I pray that they might have life, love, happiness, joy, peace, contentment, health, and health in our minds, body and spirits.

I thank You for giving all generations the blessings of giving and caring for one another. For allowing us to have courage in all things even if our words had not line up with what the Word says for our lives. I thank You for ending everything that is not of You. Lord, it is a blessing to be free and feel free of generational curses. Amen.

"The God who calleth you into eternal life, after suffering for a little while he will remold you and make you stronger and firmer."

1 Peter 5-10 says God shows undeserved kindness to everyone. This is why He appointed Christ Jesus to choose you to share in His eternal glory. You will suffer for a while, but God will make you complete; strengthen you to make you strong and firm.

Don't give up on yourself, your family and your love ones. You can break those chains that have been tormenting your family. If you believe and have faith in His Word, you will see changes in your generation. You have to pray without ceasing until you see the miracles of your love ones healed and set free.

DEDICATIONS

Dedication to My Mother, Dorothy M. Johnson

I dedicate "mother's love" to my mom, Dorothy M. Johnson, who poured into my spirit and heart pure unconditional love from childhood to adulthood. She sacrificed to make sure all of her children had what they needed. She is a beautiful mother, who I love so much, and at age 88 she stills amazes me of what she can do. She continues to give love. I pray that God extends her life beyond her years to be able to see her 5th generation and watch my grandchild, her 4th generation, Salyndria's miracle baby grow and fulfill what God purposed for him with his mom. My mother endured so much raising seven children after getting a divorced, but she made it.

God has given her sunshine and rain with her children. She never gave up on God and God never gave up on her. She instilled God's love in all her children. As stated earlier, we had rules. If you didn't go to church or school, you couldn't go out to play, no exception. She has more strength than she realized, especially when I saw her endure the loss of four children; her baby son most recently. God has given her so much strength and He walked with her during her grief, disappointments, hardship, tears, along with dealing with her own sickness. I give thanks to the Lord because through it all, she is still standing strong and running His race that is set before her at her age.

Her testimony is always, I know God is able because He brought me through many storms, sickness, and operations. I totally depend on Him especially when the doctors said no, and God said yes.

She has so many gifts and talents beyond me. Sewing and making her own clothes was one of them. But I have a little bit of this talent myself. When I was a teenager, mom made some of my clothes. She is also a great cook, and at one time in her life, she was a caterer with her sister Viola Cook-King. Also, she was a jewelry maker. For over 40 years, she taught me how to make jewelry. Often we made bracelets together. This was put into my spirit to do as I listened to a sermon from Bishop T. D. Jakes as I mentioned earlier. I thought about what he said, and I am so thankful for that message because children today don't have these conversations with their parents or grandparents so they will never know the talents and gifts that were within their parents.

My mom is such an inspiration; she even drew our family reunion t-shirts design. One time she drew abstract paintings. She did all of this while being on oxygen 24/7 in a wheelchair. She also stills goes to church with a big smile dressing up with her hats and praising the Lord. I'm so thankful for Pastor Bobby Davis for continuing the vision of the "Keenagers" for the mothers and seniors of the New Legacy Community Church in Desoto, TX. It allows them to feel wanted and still be a part of something great with the ministry.

I am also grateful for my brother Bruce for taking our mother to her church every Sunday. It's a sacrifice when you don't belong to the same church. I love him for his contribution and caring spirit for loving our mother that much to make sure she still hears the Word of God. It's a blessing for me to have him left as a brother. May God continue healing and protecting him for his vision and God's purpose. Now, my mother only have one son left, and I'm so thankful to God for keeping him.

In addition, I must say if there is anyone with a servant's heart, it's Cindy Morrow. She faithfully took my mother to church for years (every Sunday) without accepting anything in return. May blessings fall upon her. May others follow in her footsteps, so our seniors can get to church more often. Thank you, God, for the people You have surrounded me with for my mother. You gave me the perfect mom.

Does anyone know the cost of being a mother? It will cost you something. It will cost you your time, joy, peace, finances, and sometimes; your sweat and tears walking the floor at night praying unto the Lord for help and miracles. But it's worth it all to give unconditional love to a child of God who gave you the gift of life. May it be returned to mothers, the love they give out, which is the greatest gift of all. For this, I give thanks again to the Lord for positioning my mother to be my mom with so much love to give despite her circumstances. For without her, I would not be who I am today and would not be able to pour out the love that I give daily without anything in return. I love you mother!

Dedication To My Daughter, Salyndria

This is a special dedication to my only child who has always given me unconditional love. I am proud of the young lady she has become. I am so thankful to God for giving me the gift of life, my daughter. She has made a great difference in my life. She brings me joy when I am sad. She brings me peace when I am at wit's ends. She is my inspiration.

I know growing up by herself wasn't easy without her father, whom she loved so much, and the pain she felt at a young age (age 13) losing her dad to cancer. You expect your parents to be around until you are grown to witness your family and future generations, but this was not true for her. A father is so important in the household. Some may try to make excuses not to believe this, but fathers play a great roll in the family. Your daughters' relationships when they are grown have a lot to do with how they were raised and what to look for in a man. Fathers lay the foundation in their lives in education, knowledge and wisdom and what type of honorable man to look for; not just to settle. If this component is missing in their lives, it can be very difficult for young ladies seeking the right spouses for their lives.

Even though my daughter did not have her dad growing up, she made it in spite of what she had to endure (tears, suffering, disappointments, uncertainties, and circumstances beyond her control). I thank God that He was with her and was her foundation for love; guiding her through the Word.

The sacrifices she made going back to college to get her master's degree and completing it with a 4.0 grade point average. I am so proud of her accomplishments. Sure, she had setbacks from a complicated emergency C-Section giving birth to her child, and they were both hospitalized nearly three weeks, but God sustained them. I cried every day and night, but I never left the hospital without praying for my daughter. She is the most compassionate, caring, loving, kind, sweet, and lovable person with a smile that will bring sunshine into any atmosphere.

She was sent by the Lord to be a part of me and for us to push each other into greatness. For what I do in life is for her, my grandchild, and any future grandchildren to be born. It is a generational purpose for me to experience the blessings of Abraham and to cancel out every generational curse that have plagued my family by using God's Word. I am confident that God expects us to be blessed. He gave all mothers instinct to know the love between mothers and daughters, which He gave to me and my daughter -- a closeness that is truly endearing.

This is the prayer I leave for my daughter: That she would continue to pray; believing and trusting God, no matter what it looks like. Only He can heal, set free and reverse any circumstances. I pray, decree and declare over her, life blessings from above. I pray doors that have been closed for a protracted amount of time, will open up with the Lord's blessings that He has ordained for her.

New beginnings, new visions, so that she could walk in the purpose of God that He has designed for her. May opportunities come her way that seems unbelievable, and that she would know it is God opening up the windows of abundance, so she can be the best mom God has designed her to be. He gave her a son -- a blessing of life -- and He has purpose for both of them.

I want you to know, God is still walking with you, even now, as a one-year breast cancer survivor. Remember, God is still with you and He gives life no matter what the enemy tries to throw your way. Just know the love of God heals, delivers, and reverse situations and sicknesses. With miracles and His healing power; the blood that runs through your body by faith and belief, you are whole. He created you with love and created every cell, tissue, muscle, bone, vein, and organ in your body. He is the physician over all physicians in the natural. Trust Him and stand on His Word no matter what you see or experience in the natural because He heals in the spirit. He sends the Holy Spirit to minister to you from within to release change on the outside. May His angels always cover you at all times and cancel out fear. For you shall be a light for others for God's purpose that's coming behind you.

I pray that nothing will overtake you and that God will always be walking with you with His miraculous light and power. I pray you experience the joy and love only God can give. May He place you around the right Christians that will uplift and pray for you as you walk through the door, He opens for you. May He cancel out any infirmities that try to invade your body and give you health for years to come. May He continue to give you life, for His love endures forever.

Never give up because He has great things in store for you. No matter what you have been through, He still got you. Never be tricked by the adversary's lies he tries to send your way. You have been through so much and it tears me to think of all the pain you have been through. We both have cried enough tears together to sank anything that will fill water up. I love you so much, and the best is yet to come with Christ blessings He has for you. Nothing can void that because God's Word will never return void. Stay focus, positive, and renew your mind daily. God gives mercy and grace every day. Remember this always, I love you so much! Mom

Dedication To Prince - Jalen-Thomas | May 29, 2016

What a gift of life to be born. Yes, Jalen you are a gift from God. You waited and waited and struggled and struggled but held onto God's promise that you should live and not die. In your mother's womb you had many challenges; yet, you held on and was born. God knew the destiny He had for you, and that was to be born for His purpose so you could change your generation and receive the generational blessings that are outlined in the Bible. May the hand of God always be upon you.

I pray that the prayers I prayed before you were ever thought of in the flesh (my vision) and God's purpose would propel you to grow to be an anointed man of God with wisdom, knowledge, love, joy, peace, happiness, compassion, and humility. I prayed that you have understanding in all things; educated with unspeakable knowledge of whatever you do. May you have wisdom "ahead of your time" to be above.

Always "look to the hills of where your help cometh from. Your help comes from the Lord who made heaven and earth." Always remember your help comes from God, not people. If you look to people instead of God, you are setting yourself up for disappointments. Work through God's strength, not your own because you can do all things through Christ. May you stay focused and may God order your steps. And may you have the wisdom to know the difference.

I pray that God will have a hedge of protection over you, your family and your mother forever. May you always know love from your mother and father, so you may be able to give it back in return when you are in the same position as a parent or a husband.

I decree and declare you will never be broken or misused by anyone. I pray that you will know the difference of a trickster, as well as be aware of their traps. For at my age, I'm so honored to see my generation. For whatever the reason in this season, I'm so thankful for you. I want you to know that you are loved and was always loved even before you were born.

Take these words and always be kind and tender hearted, but never allow anyone to use you for their good. Be used only by God for it is His purpose that you were born. You are the fourth generation from my mom. Your great-grandmother has five generations, and believe me, it was an honor for her to still be alive to witness your birth -- your generation. Your mother loves you so much and it brings tears to my eyes just to think about what she went through just for you to be born.

Jalen, know we all love you. Make no mistake, you are very much loved. Never forget these words, love is the greatest of all, and God looks at your heart, not your titles. God knows the thoughts He thinks toward you. Thoughts of peace and not evil; and for you to have an expected end. God expects you to succeed and so do I; your grandma, Linda Gregory.

Dedication To My Sister Sharon | December 14, 2011

I dedicate this to my sister Sharon who was in a fire with her grandkids and they escaped unharmed. However, her son was still in his apartment and the smoke overtook him and synched his lungs due to smoke inhalation. Unfortunately, he was lying in the house for quite a long time, an hour or two before being removed. When he was taken out, he was unconscious. No one knew whether he was going to make it or not.

He was taken to the Burn Unit of a nearby hospital on life support. I remember calling everyone across the states and asking them to pray at a particular time for God to heal and save his life. I even asked everyone on Facebook to pray for him pleading to God myself to show up in his life and show the world that He was able to bring him out. While there was little hope, but I was told that there was an army of family and friends at the hospital crying and praying, believing that God can and will answer.

My sister was shocked with disbelief. "This can't be happening to my son," she said. One time, they had to put him in an ice bath to "break" his fever. They tried numerous times to see if he could come off life support on his own, but it was to no avail. Amazingly, when he did come off life support, there was a great witness of people present and a day later, he was able to go downstairs in the lobby as people was coming in to see him in a coma in the room.

This was truly an amazing story, and God showed up just in time for Christmas, and made a liar out of satan, the doctors, and all the onlookers who was there. I thank God for this mighty miracle that "woke up" so many people that day at the hospital of what God can do even when there is no hope.

You see, there were many people on one accord praying and God showed up and answered our prayer. This glorious resurrection day, God was in charge. His mother will never forget the miracle that was done that day. It was truly God at work sitting on the throne performing a supernatural miracle.

I Dedicated This To My Sister Sharon's Love For Her Son - Poetry

Sharon, Sharon, I know you're there, day end and day out. Oh, how it hurt, Sharon, Sharon, Sharon, oh how it hurt, Sharon, Sharon. The love you show day in and day out. Oh, how it hurt. You press through the pain and press through the darkness, knowing the love you have for your son. I pray that God will grant the both of you a second chance to see and experience God's power, and his mighty miracles. He performs regardless of what the doctor says; He is in control. Oh Sharon, Sharon, I know you're there, day end and day out, Sharon, Sharon, oh Sharon

I know you are praying fervently because of the love you feel for your son. Pressing through the pain day end and day out. You pressed your way to the hospital every day, praying, hoping, and believing in God's Word that your son would be alright. Oh Sharon, Sharon, Sharon.

Sharon, Sharon, it hurts so much to see your son lying in the hospital bed in a coma on life support. Oh Sharon, Sharon, God hadn't forgotten you. He's talking to your son as he laid in the coma making a decision of how many prayers went up to heaven on his behalf. Oh Sharon, Sharon, God hadn't forgotten your prayers. A mother's request asking for your son to live coming from his bedside. Oh Sharon, Sharon, so much love you have given as a mother with faith. Sharon, Sharon, oh Sharon.

Sharon, Sharon, oh Sharon, you and your son knows God. He watched you return to your knees. He saw you in the chapel. He saw you in the church. He saw you praying in the morning, mid-afternoon, and at night. He saw your tears at bedtime still praying for the Savior to save your son. To give you another chance with him, to give him another chance with you. God knows, and he wants you both to have another chance to get it right, oh, God, knows.

He is still talking to your son, and He's going to show the world such a great miracle. He is going to show your generation such a great supernatural miracle. So the doubters and unbelievers will witness what God can do without the doctors' help. Oh Sharon, Sharon, a mother's love for her son is undeniable powerful with unconditional love just as Christ loves you both.

Sharon, Sharon, oh how it hurt to see your son in a coma stuck on life support with pneumonia, but Sharon, Sharon, God is still talking to your son. He knows your love is real, but He wants to find out just how deep your son's love is for Him, and how bad do He wants to live. How bad do he wants to change his life.

Sharon, Sharon, everything looks dim. You son's lungs are gravely ill, but Sharon, God hasn't forgotten about you and your son and His promise to your generation. He loves you both so much that He died on the cross for a time as this. How much faith do you have He ask? Yes, He saw you pray day end and day out, but He wants to know your faith. Oh Sharon, Sharon, yes, Sharon, your faith.

Oh, how it hurt, but you press on standing on God's Word for healing for your son. Oh Sharon, Sharon, the enemy didn't count on a mother pressing to "touch the hem of His garment." Oh Sharon, Sharon, knowing that if you just touched the hem of His garment, your son would be healed miraculously. God will answer a mother's prayer for her son. Sharon, Sharon, keep believing.

Oh, son, you know your mother is praying for you wanting you to live to get a second chance. Oh, son, a mother's prayer -- praying for your life. Sharon, Sharon, Sharon, God witnessed the prayer lines, His churches of all religions praying on one accord for you. Praying on the internet; praying with families across the airwaves. Oh Sharon, Sharon, Sharon, He's been waiting for all to come together in His name. He sees your son fragile lifeless body looking hopeless in man's eyes, but He is in the midst. Oh Sharon, Sharon, oh Sharon, Sharon, Sharon, He heard your cry, saw your tears and knows your heart.

Oh Sharon, Sharon, grandma is "putting a word in" knowing the "smell of a miracle" because she's "been around the block" in sickness and unfavorable results from doctors. Oh Sharon, Sharon, Sharon, Grandma's prayers are powerful with wisdom and knowledge of God's unchanging hand.

Sharon, Sharon, God just answered your prayers. Arise son, roll the stone away. A mother's prayer just came alive. Arise son. Come forth, Jesus woke him up. God allowed the gift of life to come back into him. It was a miracle to come out of a coma and get stronger in three days and be released from the hospital without an oxygen tank.

Sharon did you hear me, no oxygen for his lungs. After him lying in the smoke for all that time breathing in black smoke being unconscious, and yet, God delivered him out of the hospital as if it never happened. He heard your prayers day and night and He gave him life again for all to see that miracles still happen as in biblical times. He is still able when you exercise your faith. We may not know who He will heal, deliver and set free, but we do know He is able so why can't it be you. Continue praying for yourself and family asking for Him to release the angels and send a miracle for your circumstances.

****

Ironically, when I wrote this for my sister in 2011, I never knew that five years later I would be doing the same thing for my daughter and grandson asking God for miracles and for people to pray around the states on one accord. I thank God for His mercy and grace for what He has done in my sister's life with her son. I also thank Him for what

He has done in my life and for the miracles, mercy and grace He has showed toward me and my family.

Never give up no matter what you have heard or witness. Don't quit on God because He won't quit on you. May my sister know the love of a sister for all I ever wanted was for her son to be healed and for restoration to take place. It was also my desire that a revival would take place in her family and other families who dealt with painful sicknesses and situations that left them numb. May God get the glory, and everyone be healed totally in their bodies. Amen!

Dedication To My Niece, Krystal

I dedicate this section to my niece who I call my daughter, Krystal. Her mother, my sister Jacqueline (Jackie) passed away. The love they had was unconditional. I had the privileged of loving her as a baby and all the way into womanhood. She is an amazing person, full of God's Spirit. I watched her grow into this beautiful positive person full of love and life to give. It amazes me the "Word" that's inside of her and the work that she does even preaching at times. May God continues to grow her and give her wisdom and knowledge. I pray God continuous covering over her and keep her healthy and blessed with miracles. May closed doors open up. May doors of opportunities and blessings fall upon you forever more. My sister may not be here, but she is watching down on her daughter seeing her growth and her accomplishments in Christ.

May mothers and daughters never experience lack again. For God shall supply all their needs according to His riches and glory in Christ Jesus.

Dedication To My Fourth Siblings Who Passed July 2017-Charles E Strickland, Sr.

You were the bright light in your mother's heart. You were my baby brother whom I loved so much that I stuck by you through all your ups and downs. Your smile will be missed, even our debates with love and compassion. Wishing I had more time to talk with you again. The years I spent with you were more precious then you realized.

The tears still fall when I think of you even in my spirit. For the grief I feel I couldn't speak because of another painful circumstance with my own, but I still thought of my brother dealing with so much pain in my family. I know God has a plan for the rest he left behind, and I know my brothers and sister are in heaven rooting and praying we make it down here on earth as well as experience God's love, provision and miracles He has for my family. The pain has been so unbearable losing love ones as if it's a plague, but I continue to pray for protection for my family. I never knew not coming by for one day I wouldn't see my brother anymore. Everyday our lives are so precious. Rest in peace, brother, I will always carry you in my heart and spirit. The sister you always said you trust with your life. Love you forever more. Rest in peace. Gone too soon.

POETRY

Drama -Why? | March 24, 2014

From the stresses of striding to be all who God said that you are, and trying to do His deed, sometimes there will be drama. On this day "drama" was put in my spirit as a poem to help someone who is going through.

Drama – Why? Poem

Why so much drama? Why so much drama? Why, why, why, do you have so much drama? Look up and look down, who do you see? Why so much drama? Why so much drama? Drama is everywhere. Everywhere there is drama.

Why so much drama? Do you know you are the creator of your drama? Did you know no one can create drama, but the drama queen or king? Do you know who you are or whose you are? Why so much drama? When you go to sleep at night do you know you have a keeper? Yes, a keeper of the all times high, who stoop low and pick you up to an all-time high. So why, why tell me why are there so much drama? Why when you have a creator who can reach down while you are in your drama and "snatch" the attitude, frustration, anger, lying spirit, and foolishness right from you and cancel out all that drama that got you stuck in life because you are dealing with too much negativity that has created a lifestyle of drama. Do you know who you are?

Why, why so much drama all the time. I said why, why so much drama all the time. Why, why do you hurt the people who love you so much? I said why, why so much drama all the time. I said why, why so much drama all the time?

Why do you have so much anger in your spirit? Why are you angry when you have people God sent to be at your side? Why, why do you try to run them away from you? With actions of frustration and pain. Did you know people love you? So why, why do you try to run people away that God sent to hold you up? Why, when He sent the love ones who cares, what happens to you?

So why, why so much drama all the time? Why do you lash out with so much pain in your words to the ones God sent who understands your plight? So why, why so much drama all the time. Why so much drama all the time. God knows your pain. He heard your sound as a roaring lion deep down in your gut. So why so much drama? He saw you looking down in the darkest places; yet, He is still walking with you. So why so much drama? So much drama, so much drama. Don't you know He is Alpha and Omega? The healer, the Lilly of the valley, the Morning Star, and the Finisher of your faith. He is the only One who can change your circumstances. Let Him in and appreciate the love ones He has orchestrated to be at your side. So, no more drama.

He cares and loves you so much. He took away your pain. He put you up toward the sky, back on your feet. Why so much drama? Why, why be confused when He renewed your mind. Tell me why, why so much drama? Look inside of you, open up your ears to hear Him. Look around, you are not alone. He is all around you in the morning, noonday and night. When you cannot see your way through just know He is in the midst. So why so much drama, my brothers and sisters? Why? It doesn't have to be so much drama because He is right there in the drama to bring you out. So why so much drama Why so much drama?

Sometimes in life people are consumed with so much drama that they have lost sight of where God was trying to take them. Some people have such a negative spirit that only God can heal them because nothing you say will ever convince them that they are "drama." The stresses of life can bring so much drama especially when we find ourselves so lost in our lives with our families (and children) situations that every word becomes conflict and drama.

Sometimes even your friends can cause so much drama in your life, not knowing they got issues from their past. I pray for healing for all who need a second touch from God.

Who is sick of the drama and just want out of drama to live a free-spirited loving life without dysfunction and people contributing into what you are already facing?

No more drama, you can be drama free to live mentally, physically, emotionally, spiritually, and financially free. Amen

A Brother's Anger

After watching so many brothers walk around with anger issues, I decided I had to write this poem because so many brothers have pain turned inside out while crying out for help, but they will not admit they need healing. I wrote this poem to reach the brothers that are in so much pain and needs to know someone cares. If this applies to you, may you be healed, and feel free enough to reach out for help, so you may live the life that God has for you.

A Brother's Anger Poem

Brother, because of disappointments, frustration, hurt, pain, you became wrapped up in bitterness and anger. Brother, look what you've done to yourself, your spirit, your soul. You have allowed negativity and pain to drain you because of disappointments in life. Unforeseen negative circumstances and things knowingly caused by you now are upon you as a chain by the adversary. A brother's anger.

Brother, I sing about a brother's anger because so many brothers have become bitter, bitter, bitter, bitter, wrapped up in bitterness and anger. Yes brother, I sing about their minds and how they become what God said they were not. A brother's anger, a brother's anger, I sing a brother's anger.

Brother, why are you so bitter? You've taken your past hurts, disappointments, frustration, pain, and negative thoughts and allowed them to filter down into your spirit. Turning your mind into something that is not of God. Brother's anger, that's why I sing, a brother's anger. Instead of venting all the time about who's who or what someone subjected you to, which turned into more anger, brother, brother, why a brother's anger.

Brother, don't you know your anger have turned love ones from you because of your bitterness. Brother, why. This is why I sing a brother's anger. A brother's anger, a brother's anger, a brother's anger, brother, why, a brother's anger.

Brother, did you stop to think why your love ones hasn't left you? They understand your pain, your frustration, sickness, disappointments, discouragements, loneliness, desertion, brother, why? This is why I sing a brother's anger, yes, a brother's anger.

Brother, they're there when you're venting. They're there when you lash out at them. They're there when your drinks become too many. Brother, they never left you because they love you. This is why I sing a brother's an-

ger. This is why I sing, a brother's anger, yes, a brother's anger.

Who can deal with a brother's anger wrapped up in a bad attitude? Who can deal with a brother's hateful words to the ones who love him? A brother's anger, yes, a brother's anger. Who can deal with a brother's anger who turns words into pain? Who can turn a positive into a negative, a brother's anger, yes, a brother's anger?

Brother, brother, brother, your anger has become so out of control that you no longer recognize love. You're a broken man from the past who have allowed obstacles of the enemy take over your life. Yes, a brother's anger, a brother's anger, yes, a brother's anger.

Brother, brother, brother, why don't you recognize the ones standing in the gap for you? Why, why, why, don't you recognize that the pain you're feeling can turn around just by showing a little bit of love to the ones who is trying to help you into recognizing what God has for you is for you. No matter who hurt you, no matter who left you, no matter how little you progressed, and no matter of all the obstacles you may think you have. A brother's anger, yes, a

*brother's anger, why, why, yes, a brother's an-
ger, yes, a brother's anger.*

*Nevertheless, brother love is more powerful
than your anger if you allow God to heal your
brokenness. Heal that pain, mend your heart.
Bring back newness into your spirit and life.
Brother, why? A brother's anger, why, brother,
why? Yes, a brother's anger, a brother's anger,
yes, a brother's anger.*

*Brother one last chance to get it right. Take the
love. Take the advice from caring people. Take
the advice God has given you in your spirit. Just
listen to the right voice, and not the one of the
adversary -- the negative voice -- you can't go
far on negativity. It will drown you, shut your
mind down, and it will take over the love turning it into negativity. Brother, why, a brother's
anger.*

*A brother's anger, yes, a brother's anger can't
see his future from the blind eyes Satan has put
before him. Brother, open your eyes to see your
future. You do have a promising future full of
love, joy, happiness, laughter, companionship,
but, brother, you have to rid yourself of all that
anger to have love. You have to give love, and
remember, brother, the ones that don't give*

back in the end wasn't for you in the first place. That's why God had to take you "around the fence," so you could see yourself in all that pity having a party by yourself. Brother, why not choose life. He gives it just for the asking and never have to question his love for you because the past is just the past, brother's anger. Brother, why? God has given you another chance. He said it doesn't matter how many times you were knocked down. Just get up. A brother's anger. Why brother, why not choose God? A brother's anger, why brother, why not choose God and receive your peace -- a brother's anger, a brother's anger, a brother's anger. Why a brother's anger.

Where's the Peace | November 9, 2011

Peace is what everyone is searching for and need in their life, and in their mind, spirit, and emotions. If not, they will be affected mentally, physically, emotionally and spiritually. There were times when I would ask myself, "Where is the peace," because if it was not this; it was something else, and it never seemed to end.

Sometimes when life hits you hard you are pushed to be created in all areas that you never thought you had. But God knew adversity would push you to do what He intended You to do in your pain. My thoughts of my pain turning inside out caused me to petition God for help. He brought out of me what was already inside of me while asking where is the peace that surpasses all understanding? So I jotted down my thoughts and wrote the poem below.

Where's the Peace Poem

Where has it gone? Where is the peace? I remember the joy, peace, and happiness once, but where has it gone? I used to giggle like a happy little girl when we all got to together as one. Yet, when I look back, was there really peace? I remember all too well wondering what we would all look like as we age, but where's the peace? When I reflect back was there any real peace in the atmosphere, or was it just pretend? Where's the peace?
It seems so happy and felt so real to be in a

family full of laughter, smiles, jokes, so where is the real peace? What happened? When frustration, stress, anxiety, anger, sickness, illness came, then came sadness, tears and depression throughout generations. Where's the peace?

Did our peace, which were happier days, with laughter and smiles turn into tears of sickness and diseases (emphysema, heart disease, diabetes, cancer, liver disease, congested heart failure, etc.), along with failed relationships; pain on top of pain, emotional unbalance, suicidal thoughts, depression on top of depression. What happened to the peace? Where's the peace?

Did we miss all understanding? Love is peace. Love is God. God is love. Love is beauty, Love is calmness. Love is happiness and joy. Love is knowing when you are in the wrong company. Love is hearing God's voice. Love is a bundle of peace, so where's the peace?

Why did we come together with so much mistrust and negativity, but this is not what matters? God matters because He is the only One who can give you peace that surpasses all understanding. Where is the peace?

Come back together with God's love and you will find the peace that is missing out of your spirit. Come back to God's Word and you will find His love that only He can give. Come back to God's Word and the love, peace, happiness, and joy that He gives. Come back to the light on your knees. Day and night, you will find God. You will find the peace you have lost.

Lose the anger, lose the violence, lose the alcoholism, lose the lies, and lose the disrespect. Lose the hatred, lose the family arguments, lose the lust, and lose the low self-esteem. Lose the bitterness and lose the enemies in your life that's turning you from God. Where's the peace? Lose the cheating, lose the lying, and lose the complaining spirit. Where's the peace. Lose the bickering, where's the peace. Lose the mistrust, lose the low self-esteem. Where is the peace?

Love, love, love, love like it's the love of your life, but it's Jesus. Just test Him and see if He'll give you your peace back. Just trust Him and see if you receive the peace that surpasses all understanding. Try Jesus and see how much peace you will receive. Trust Jesus and let your spirit find its peace. Trust Jesus and let the Holy Spirit convict you of the right ways of life.

Trust Jesus and get your mind back. Get your heart right. Take off that bitterness and find humility. Break down the generational curses of sickness, disease, mental health, and lack of financial increase. Bring God back into your life, as well as your family and your children. Receive the blessings of Abraham generationally and get your peace back. Know where the peace is. It is inside of you by finding God. Peace, peace, peace, peace, where is God and the peace you were promised. Where is God? Find Him and you will find your peace. Where's the peace? Where's the peace?

I Believe | December 6, 2010

It was on December 6, 2010, that I kept telling myself, "I believe even when nothing seems to change." I still kept telling myself, "I believe things are going to get better and I knew no matter how many years it would take, I still had to hold onto my belief and faith in God." As I was thinking about belief, I kept writing until it made sense to me. I had to put it in my spirit and pray that one day even if I can reach one or two that they will believe also. That they will believe that all things are possible to those who believe.

I Believe Poem

I believe in hopes and dreams. Oh, I believe. Oh, I believe in my hopes and dreams. Yes, I believe. I believe, I believe, I believe, I believe in my hopes and dreams. Yes, I believe. I believe that I was set free to do God's will. Oh, I believe. I believe I was set free to do God's will. Oh, I believe. Oh, I believe. Da de da, I believe. Oh, da de da, I believe. Yes, I believe.

I believe in the power that I was given. Oh, I believe. Yes, I believe, I believe, I believe. Yes, I believe. Yes, I believe in the power that I was given. Oh, yes, I believe.

I was still one night, and I heard that silent voice inside my spirit from God saying, "You better believe, you better believe. I didn't die on the cross for you not to believe. Yes, you better believe. I didn't die on the cross for you not to believe."

Oh ah da de da de da, I believe. Oh, da de da, I believe. He gave me hope and dreams in a cup of faith. Just in case I don't believe. Oh yes, He put it in a bowl of hope. Oh yes, I believe. Yes, I believe. When I looked up towards the sky and saw the beautiful rainbow, so many colors it was a vision of hope and dreams that God put for me to see. My spirit came alive. Look up, not down, look to the heavens where your help come from. Oh, I believe. Yes, I believe, I believe.

That mustard seed of a cup of faith, and that bowl of hope. Oh, oh, I believe. Yes, I believe. I believe. You better believe because He died on the cross for you and me. Just open your eyes and believe what He put inside of you. Yes, I believe. Oh, I believe, I believe. He died on the cross for my hopes and dreams to come to light. Yes, I believe. Yes, I believe, I believe.

Wake up out of your coma and believe and get back focus on the gifts He put on the in-

side of you. Yes, I believe. Do you believe? Yes, I believe. Yes, I believe. Wipe those tears and believe, stay away from the negativity and believe. Put that smile back on your beautiful face and believe. Wipe those tears away and believe. Yes, I believe, I believe. Touch your heart and believe. Yes, I believe, I believe, I believe. Yes, I believe, I believe.

He's just a whisper away if you call Him. He didn't die on the cross for you not to believe. You better believe, you better believe, yes, I believe, I believe, I believe. Yes, I believe, I believe, I believe, I believe. Yes, I believe.

Are You Confused? | November 11, 2011

Sometimes you can misread a person and find out they aren't who you think they are because of so much confusion and dysfunction in their lives. Some people are mentally confused, and some are just confused because of what they went through; therefore, they have lost their joy, and they don't know their purpose.

Confusion, confusion, how can I find myself again. You can be so confused from hearing too many people and voices, which can lead you in the wrong direction. Or are we just confused because we don't understand ourselves. I am always writing down what I think and what God puts into my spirit. On certain days I would just write.

Are You Confused Poem

Confusion, confusion, confusion, are you confused? Confusion, confusion, confusion.

Do you misinterpret matters of your life? Confusion, confusion, confusion. If you do, you are confused. Confusion, confusion, confusion, confusion.

When you speak, do you always feel you are being misjudged? Talk about being misunderstood. Confusion, confusion, confusion, confusion, why are you confused?

Are you confused? Confusion, confusion, confusion, confusion. Lord, just confused. Confusion, confusion, confusion, confusion, mentally confused, purposely confused. Confusion, confusion, confusion, confusion. Are you confused?

Confusion, confusion, confusion, confusion, yes, confusion all the time. I hear you, but I'm confused on the matters of life. Yes, you said it. I misread myself and everyone else all the time. Am I confused? Or maybe it just looks that way. Well, Lord, confusion, confusion, confusion, confusion, confusion. Just plain confused.

Love is joy. Love is smiling knowing inside you, you are smiling with the Lord in your spirit. I dare you to have joy. Yes, why be confused? I dare you to have joy. Why don't you know the matters of your life? I dare you to have joy, peace, love from within. Confusion, confusion, confusion.

Joy comes in the morning, joy comes in the middle of the day; joy comes at night. I dare you to have joy. Never let someone steal your joy and make you think or feel you're confused. Confusion, confusion, confusion, con-

fusion. Yes, don't be confused. I dare you to unravel the confusion. I dare you to take back your joy, peace, love, and happiness. Confusion, confusion, confusion, confusion. Get your mind back. Get your life back. Get your spirit back. Get your soul back. Get everything that God has given you back.

Get your smile back. I dare you to have joy again. I dare you to have peace again. I dare you to walk with God again. I dare you to get back to the altar, so you won't be confused.

Stop this confusion. Stop this confusion. None of it is from God. God didn't make His children confused. This is from the enemy who come to steal, kill and take your thoughts -- confuse your mind. Free your spirit. It's a state of confusion, confusion, confusion. Get your mind back and unleashed all the confusion in your life. Get back to the joy of the Lord. I said get back to the joy of the Lord. Dare yourself to get back up again. I dare you to get back up again and receive your peace. Confusion, confusion, confusion.

Deep thought-brothers' uncaring spirit | March 21, 2014

I have dealt with so many brothers that have been hurt and their spirits are damaged, and they don't realize that the pain they feel have left a void in them, and therefore, it has damaged relationships they are connected to (marriages, families, friends, co-workers, acquaintances, etc.). It is sad because of their uncaring spirit, people cannot get close to them to find the real person inside. I had to write this section because this touched me with brothers that have so much anger in them that they snap at their love ones all the times. They don't care what you say or try to do for them, so I wanted these brothers to know, not everyone is against them. The people that God has placed in their lives are there for them, but their spirits are so uncaring that they are running them away and ruining their own lives. And if they don't stop doing this, then eventually they will find themselves alone in life. There is help for you, but first you have to accept that something is wrong inside of you that caused you to have that uncaring spirit full of anger.

Brothers' Uncaring Spirit Poem

Lord, Lord, Lord, what have I done to deserve an uncaring brother whose spirit is broken. Why must I waste my years of happiness worrying over his uncaring spirit. Oh, Lord, why do he not see that Your hand is in the middle of his life? No matter what I do it does not matter to him. It's just temporary, Lord. It's just temporary. Why must I give up so much to uncaring spirits? Brother, brother, an uncaring spirit.

Oh why, oh why can't he see what he has done to me? Oh why, oh why, Lord, You told me to look after him. But, Lord, why, oh why, did he take advantage of your helper that you sent. Lord, why? Oh, Lord, do I keep praying for him with my unconditional love. Oh, Lord, he took me for granted for helping him, sometimes not knowing because of an uncaring spirit. Brother, brother, you have an uncaring spirit, and yet don't realize it because of so much past pain. Brother, brother, your uncaring spirit.

Lord, why do I have a caring spirit? I give on purpose -- giving to people who don't care about themselves. It's just a temporary fix. A temporary fix, but I know you're still with him and others. Lord, I just want him to know the unconditional love you put inside of me is for him. Why, brother, why -- an uncaring spirit; the help God sent is for you. You can't see the help God has orchestrated to be by your side in time of need. Brother why, brother, why? An uncaring spirit.

Oh, Lord, why, why can't people see you as I do? Why can't my brother see You that way, too? It's like a cloud that keep covering his mind. And I pray to have that cloud removed so he can see what I see. Your hand on him, brother, why, brother, why, an uncaring spirit.

Why brother, why can't you see His hand on you, why brother, why? Why can't you open your eyes before it's too late? So, I pray just like all the other caring people whom God place in front of another to care for, brother, why. This is why I sing. Brother why? Uncaring spirit.

Lord, I ask, just give me my instructions, so I won't overload myself through giving of myself to uncaring spirits. Brother, why? Brother, why? Uncaring spirit.

Prayer For Uncaring Spirit

I pray for everyone who is trying their best to take care of a love one or person that God has placed in their hands who hasn't been cooperative. But regardless, your love still exists, and you are standing in faith that God will touch, heal and change their spirits to a much kinder and gentle caring spirit. May the frustration you feel be alleviated so you may think clearly in the time of need. May God renew your spirit so you will be capable of doing the job He set before you. May the pain that all of these brothers feel be cancelled out. Some lost themselves years ago from no fathers, no love, no relationships, no families, no under-standing, no jobs, so they became distant and disconnect-ed from their families. They lost their compassion, so they are consumed with bitterness only now for sickness to fall upon them, and now taking advantage of probably the only ones that are willing and able to help. I pray for them that they become stronger in the Word and receive their healing. I pray that you know that God did not tell you to overload yourself, so that you are stressed out trying to do what one might think impossible at times. May your family be blessed. May God provide for them what they need so everyone can take a rest to re-group themselves.

May the issues of the brothers' past be dealt with, so they may move on and be healed, delivered and set free. May they know you love them unconditionally, otherwise, you would be doing other things for yourselves instead of tak-ing care of them. I pray that they don't give up on them-

selves, and that they know that help is near through the Word of God. May God allow them to slow down and renew their spirit and mind. May God send financial support to help in all ways, so that the caregiver may be able to care for their love ones without stress, and that they would have the lifestyle that God said they could have regardless of their situation. He got you and His Word will never return void if you believe.

Brother, He's Real Poem | March 27

Brother, why do you sink so low. I know you have been through it all in your life. People disappointed you; betrayed you. You disappointed yourself and now you are sinking in your pain. Your feelings are all emotional from your past wishing you can do it all over again. Brother, just know, don't give up on yourself. It ain't over. God sees your tears in your darkest hour. He sees your loneliness. Brother, He's real. He's real. He knows this is not what you expected in life. Brother, He's real. He's real. He knows you never had the strength to lift yourself up. Brother, He's real. He's real.

The painful spirit still lingers from your past; damaged and bruised from what you had to face in your younger years. Issues from childhood (pain from your father, pain from being rejected, and pain from bad relationships). Disappointed from not being able to see your children, some, it was no fault of your own, you just couldn't make it. Nevertheless, they still need your presence. Brother, He's real. He's real. I'm here brother. I know you never had the strength to lift yourself up. Your strength is gone, but brother, He's real. He's real.

The pain is real. The loneliness is real. The sickness is real, but your story isn't over. Brother, He's real. He's real.

The sun will come out again and shine upon you, just don't give up because brother, He's real. He's real.

I know if you touch and agree with that mustard seed faith, you will be healed emotionally, spiritually, mentally, and financially in God's timing. For the blessings and miracles are still here to access through faith. Brother, He's real. He's real.

Look up brother, I never left you. I just need you to understand that I was just the messenger. God sent me to help you. Know He is real. You can have what you say, brother. Renew your mind. Brother, He's real. He's real.

Wake up out of that slumber, He is real. You can overcome that tormented mind that Satan has left upon you from not believing in God's Word entirely. Brother, He's real.

Don't Take It Personal

We all go through adversities in life and sometimes fool-ishness, but you got to let it go for your own happiness or you will lose everything and everyone that matters in your life. I began to write this poetry letter to myself about don't take it personal in 2014. It's not your problem, it's theirs, is what I heard. May this help and encourage someone to know to let it go and stop taking everything personal. It's not your problem, you have been too consumed with everyone else's problem, therefore, you took it on as yours. You can't change people only God can. Free yourself and don't take it personal.

Don't take it personal Poem | March 21, 2014

Look up, look down, what do you see? Do you see the sky awaiting the sunshine, or downward to the ground a deserted place? Don't take it personal.

When I experienced the darkness of loneliness. Don't take it personal. When the sky is no longer blue my eyes adjusted to grey. Don't take it personal.

When the emptiness began to feel like an empty nest. Don't take it personal. When my heart has pain feeling like childbirth. Don't take it personal. When anger and frustration filled my mind up un-

til it has overloaded itself into the unknown, I have never seen before. Don't take it personal.

When help come and you let it go without a thought of saying, "Lord, I need you." Don't take it personal. When our eyes meet, and I feel sadness from within. Look into my eyes and know I am no longer there. I've moved to another post office box. Don't take it personal.

When all I have felt, all I have done, all I have endured, and I can't stand the misery any longer. Don't take it personal. When the love you used to show me vanished in the air. When the laughter turned into a smudged face. Don't take it personal.

When help come to lift you up and you kept refusing the help and took advantage of the helper. Don't take it personal. When God reached out and I grabbed His hand to run His race instead of your uncomfortable nightmare of an unknown love I never had nor felt. Don't take it personal.

Because I wanted and needed God's love, not a temporary fixture of love that was fake and not real. Don't take it personal.

Just know God delivered me "federal express" to a new location in my mind, body, spirit, emotionally, mentally and physically. Don't take it personal. Where love was in the box; joy, peace, happiness, and kindness were wrapped up waiting for the right address. Don't take it personal.

Anger, frustration, lies, confusion, dysfunction, betrayal, and sadness were not wrapped inside the box. Just God's unchanging hand of love and peace. Don't take it personal. God just relocated me to a permanent address -- His. I've just moved on. Don't take it personal.

After Thought – Don't Take It Personal

This poem, I hope, will give encouragement to people who been through the fire, and have allowed people to take advantage of them. They had issues from their past -- their childhood or young adult life. People may have disappointed you. Relationships may have gone bad, and you endured a lot of pain from it whether you are a man or women. I just want you to know, don't take it personal. Just move on and let all the drama go so you can have the blessings and miracles you deserve (another chance without being offended because of what happened in your life), so you won't take it into new relationships. It will be alright. Change the way you think, and you will see the difference by doing and thinking differently. Don't take it personal.

SONGS

Power in the Word Song | January 2010

There is power in the Word
There is power in the praise
There is power in the mouth if you just open it up and praise
the Lord

There is power in the Word
There is power in the praise
There is power in your mouth if you just open it up and thank
the Lord

There is power in the Word
There is power in the praise
There is power in your mouth if you just open it up and wor-
ship the Lord

Power in the Word
Power in the Word
Power in the Word
Power in the Word
Oh, Lord, power in the Word

There is power in the Word
There is power in your praise
There is power in your mouth if you just open it up and praise
the Lord

With power of the Word anxiety got to disappear
Depression got to drop off you mentally
Suicide got to leave your thoughts and mind
Heart attacks got to be reversed; be healed and made
whole

Oh, God, there is power in the Word
Oh, God, there is power in the Word
There is power in your praise, oh God, power, power, power

Demons tremble from Your power in the Word
Blood pressure drops from Your power in the Word
Confusion disappears from Your power in the Word
Oh, Lord, there is power in the Word
Power in the Word

Restoration comes back from the power of the Word
Deliverance takes place from the power of the Word
There is power in the Word
There is power in your praise
Oh, God, there is power in the Word
Peace of mind is received from the power of the Word
Mental stability is restored from the power of the Word

Oh, yes, God, we thank You for Your power and Your Word
We thank You for allowing us by choice to rest in Your Word.
For we want change, oh, God
We thank You for there is power in the Word

There is power in Your praise
Looking up praising You for the power in the Word
Power in the Word
Power in your praise
Oh, Lord, there is power in the Word

Prayer

I praise Your name, Lord. I thank You for Your grace and mercy. I thank You for watching over all of us. I just got to praise You. I thank You for Your promise. I thank You for Your glory. I thank You for holding us and lifting us up out the hands of the enemy. I thank You for being an on time God forever more because it could have had no ending, but You stretch Your hands out and pulled my family back into safety with an amazing healing of Your grace, mercy and miracle working power. I just have to praise Your name, Christ Jesus. Hallelujah, Amen!

He Gives Me Strength Song | November 13, 2010

Me and my God
He gives me strength day by day
He gives me strength

Me and my God
He gives me strength day by day
He gives me strength

Me and God
He gives me strength day by day
He gives me strength

Me and my God
He gives me strength day by day
He gives me strength

Me and my God
He gives me strength night by night
He gives me strength

My God, He gives me strength
Oh, Lord, me and my God
He loves me so
Oh, He loves me still
He loves me so

Me and my God night by night
He gives me strength day by day; night by night
He gives me strength
Yet another day He gives me strength

Me and my God
He gives me strength
Oh, He gives me strength

Me and my God
He gives me strength in the morning, noon, and night
Me and my God
He gives me strength

Me and my God
He gives me strength
Oh, yes, He gives me strength in the midnight
He gives me strength

When I'm walking the floor at night, He gives me strength
When I'm distressed, He gives me strength
When I don't know what to do, me and my God, He gives
me strength

Me and my God
He gives me strength
Oh, yes, He gives me strength

Me and my God
He gives me strength
Yes, another day
Oh, victory is mine

Me and my God
He gave me strength
Me and my God
Yes, me, and my God

Sometimes when life is hard you think you are all alone. It is in these moments, you have to speak the Word of God into the atmosphere to give you strength to believe in your own words. I found myself needing to do this on October 24, 2009. I began to decree what I believed out loud that a song rose up in my spirit.

I Decree What I Believe Song | October 9, 2009
I decree what I believe
Oh, I decree what I believe
See yourself as God sees you
See yourself whole as God sees you
I decree what I believe

I decree what I believe
I decree what I believe
See yourself healed as God sees you
See yourself healed as God sees you
I decree what I believe

I decree what I believe
I decree what I believe
Oh, I see myself delivered from frustration and anger
I see myself as God sees me
I see myself as God sees me
I decree what I believe
I decree what I believe
I decree what I believe

I see myself happy; full of love and life
I see myself as God sees me
I see myself as God sees me
Oh, I decree what I believe

I decree what I believe
I decree what I believe
I decree my life changed for the good
I decree my life changed for the good
I decree blessings upon me because God said so
Oh, I see myself as God sees me
Oh, I see myself as God sees me
I decree what I believe

I decree what I believe
I decree what I believe
I decree generational curses broken in my family
I decree what I believe
I decree what I believe

I decree that depression is canceled out of my life
I decree sickness out of my body, mind and spirit
I decree that a victim mentality is gone forever more
Oh, I decree what I believe

I see myself as God sees me
*I see myself as God sees me -- whole and healthy (mentally,
physically, emotionally and financially)*
Oh, I believe, and I decree what God has spoken over my life

I see myself as God sees me
I decree what I believe

I decree what I believe
I decree what I believe
No more anger, no more depression
No more fear, I am filled with the Holy Spirit
Yes, I decree and believe what God said about me
Free indeed, yes, I decree what I believe
I decree what I believe
I decree what I believe

Oh, I believe what God said about me
I'm a child of God and I believe in Him; He shall set me free
Yes, I believe what God said
I believe what God said
Now, I'm free
Oh, yes, I believe
Yes, I believe
Oh, yes, I believe
I believe

Thankful Thankful Song | March 10, 2011

Lord I'm so thankful
Lord, I'm so thankful
Lord, I'm so thankful
Lord, I'm so thankful
Lord, I'm so thankful
I'm so thankful, Lord

Lord, You saved me today
Lord, You delivered me today
Lord, You kept me today
Oh, Lord, I'm so thankful
Lord, I'm so thankful
Lord, I'm so thankful
Lord, I'm so thankful
Lord, I'm just so thankful
I'm so thankful, Lord.

Lord, I thought it was over
I started giving into depression
I start wavering
Yes, I'm so thankful
Lord, I'm so thankful
Lord, I'm so thankful
Lord, I thank You for holding me
Lord, I'm so thankful

I could have lost my mine
But You held me, Lord
I'm just so thankful, Lord
I'm so thankful

Oh, Lord, I'm so thankful
So, so thankful, Lord
Oh, Lord, I'm so thankful
Lord, I'm so thankful
Lord, I looked up and down and couldn't find You
Oh, Lord, You found me
Oh, Lord, You found me
I'm so thankful, Lord

Oh, Lord, I'm so thankful
Lord, I'm so thankful
That you caught me before it was too late
Lord, I'm just so thankful
Lord, I'm so thankful
Yes, Lord, I'm so thankful
I'm so thankful, Lord

Oh, Lord, I'm so thankful
I found you today, Lord
Now, I have my spirit back
Oh, Lord, now I got my mind back from the adversary
Oh Lord, I'm so thankful

Today, You saved me, Lord
I'm just so thankful
I'm so thankful, Lord
Yes, I'm so thankful, Lord
Lord, I'm so thankful
That you saved me from myself, Lord
Yes, I'm so thankful, Lord

I'm so thankful, Lord
I thank You, Lord, for all You did in protecting me from
myself because the enemy thought he had me and You
reached out Your hand and pulled me in
Lord, I'm so thankful
Lord, I'm so thankful
Lord, I'm so thankful

Today, I'm so thankful, Lord
Lord, I'm just so thankful
I'm so thankful, Lord
I'm so thankful, Lord

My song To My Grandson

Granny got you
Granny got you
Granny got you
Granny, Granny

Granny got you
Granny got you
Granny got you
Granny, Granny

Granny got you
Granny got you
Granny got you
Just like Christ got His children

Jesus loves you
Jesus loves you
Jesus loves you
Just like Christ loves His children

Granny got you
Granny got you
Granny got you
After Granny got you
Jesus got you, Jesus got you, Jesus got you
Just like Christ got you in His hands

And are covering you
Granny love is unconditional
As it is with Christ
He loves you unconditional
Remember, Granny got you
And Christ is holding you as a child

Love forever!
Grandma

Linda's Belief in Self, Courage and Faith Chart
November 2010

B...........best is yet to come
E..........encourage yourself
L...........living for the Lord
I...........ingesting positive thoughts
E..........empower yourself
V...........visibility
E...........endure

I...........inventing new ideas
N..........new beginnings

S...........self awareness
E...........expectation of the blessings from God
L.............let foolish things go that is not from God
F...........faith is the center of my life

C..........covering for your love ones
O..........obtaining wisdom
U..........understanding the Word
R..........relinquishing fear
A..........attitude change
G...........greatness in your mind
E..........experiencing God's unconditional love

F...........following the Word
A..........always in the Word
I............in sync with the Word
T..........taking your life back
H..........healing in the Word

Who Are Your Angels?

My grandmother always told me I could do anything if I put my mind to it, and I can always do better no matter what your better was regardless what road I chose. She told me God was taking me places and He has His hand on my life.

I remember when I was in my 20's or so, I was driving alongside a road and I stopped at a traffic light where there was a bus stop. I remember this elderly lady spoke to me at the light while I was waiting for it to change. I had the window down and she said, "You're the chosen one and you shall be blessed." I smiled and said, "Thank you," asking myself why would she say that? I turned for a quick second to see if the light had changed so I could proceed and when I looked back, she was gone as if I was talking to a ghost. I said to myself that old lady could not have ran up the street and there was nothing distracting me from seeing her walk away, so this was strange.

I looked up and down the street, but I saw no one. I said to myself no one could disappear this fast at least not at her age. Later on, I told my mom what I experienced, but I did not tell anyone else because they probably will think I lost my mind.

No one can vanish in thin air for a second; I kept telling myself. The bus never came, and she surely did not get on it and no one drove by because it was just me sitting at the light. I'm still puzzle today about the incident. My mom said to me you were visited by an angel. That's why you didn't see her again. She delivered a message from God to you and that was it. I always said to myself, "Yeah, she was right. I surely was chosen to suffer, so I don't know how chosen I was." You never know who are the angels in your life? Some are sent to deliver a message, and some are in the natural sent to help you in distress. Who are your angels?

Dedication to William D. Watley

I received the foundation of the Word of God in my life when I became a member of St. James A.M.E church in Newark, NJ under Rev. William D. Watley. He taught and preached the Word of God whereby anyone could comprehend it. He inspired me so much when he taught on being a visionary. I remember him teaching on visionaries so well that he had a conference called "Visionary." I took my mom, and after this, God spoke to me to relocate from New Jersey when the time was right. I did, and my mother came with me.

Rev. Watley made it so clear about a visionary and who you should only tell. Yes, only another visionary. He said, if you tell your vision to someone that's not a visionary, he/she could block your blessings by putting doubt in your mind and causing you to rethink what God had already planted in your spirit. Be careful who you speak your plans to. I remember this so well. Plus, sometimes you may have to go alone if no one wants to follow. Everyone is not ordained to go with you. You may have to go by yourself if no one else has a desire to see your vision. Your vision is for you, but sometimes the people connected to you get blessed by being connected to you. I have no regrets because Rev. Watley was so right. I have learned that people don't always agree with your dreams and visions because it's above their heads. They think it won't happened, but keep dreaming, planning and asking God for wisdom, knowledge, and be patience until you see the manifestation. The doubters will know God is so real and He keeps His Word. What's for you has your name on it only. Thank you so much, Rev. Watley for what you poured into my spirit to set the stage for me to rethink my life for change. I will always love you for that great teaching I was under, especially Hour of Power Bible Study at 11 a. m., and the short sermon following. He would bless the people with lunches afterward. May God continue blessing and raising him up.

A Pastor Who Poured Into My Spirit And Life
Rest In Peace Rev. Robert Kent

This man I love so much because he had a servant's heart; he touched everyone. I call him my spiritual mentor, The Late Rev. Robert Kent from St. James A.M.E. church in Newark, NJ. He had the heart of pure love and the anointing of God's spirit on him. He always was there for me. I remember every Wednesday afternoon after Bible study, I would go to the altar for prayer. Religiously, I did this. One day he instructed me to write everything down on a sheet of paper and bring it to the altar after service, and he would pray with me to allow God to break every stronghold that was pulling on me to stop me where God was taking me. He did, and we went over every request I wrote down, then we gave it to God. He anointed my forehead and both my hands. I remember tearing up because I was in so much pain whereby I could not speak about it to no one but him.

In his ministry, he prayed for the sick and he took it very seriously. Nothing was fake about him. He truly was called to do God's work. I have never met anyone like him. He would stop you in the crowd, leaving out of the church, to pray for you. In the parking lot, he would stop and pray for you. This man I love so much.

He prayed for everyone in my family. He would call me up and pray for me. If I would tell him my mother was sick, he would call her. There were times she could hardly breathe, but he never stopped praying over the phone until her breathing got better. I would always say The Late Rev. Kent would pray you well if you weren't. He stood strong on the Word and would tell me to anoint everything including my door post in the house to kick the adversary out. Yes, he was that kind of man of God. He is the one person I wish I could have reached back and blessed because he deserved all of God's blessings for what he has done for everyone who was sick, distressed, frustrated and in the hospital or home sick. He will never be forgotten.

When I relocated to Texas from New Jersey, he called me and said, "Listen carefully, God gave me a word for you. I want you to hear it well and I want you to listen clearly what I have to say," and I did. I remember saying wow what is this. He said God said, "The baton is in your hand now, and you're standing in the gap of your generation."

For years I have been trying to figure out what it meant. Eventually, I figured it out. I always pray generationally and always pray to break generational curses in my family, so now I understand about the baton. When I come out, my family comes out generationally. I also prayed for generational blessings to be released in my family. They shall come to pass. Rev. Robert Kent, it was a sincere honor to be in your presence with the healing word always. You will never be forgotten, RIP.

Recognition to Bishop T. D. Jakes

I can't say enough about this anointed man of God who I'm proud to sit under his teachings and word from God, Bishop T. D. Jakes. He doesn't know it, but he has inspired me to reach for my goals. He speaks to my spirit and pushes me to keep doing better; searching and pulling out what God put inside of me every time I go to church. I have never been pushed liked I have out of my comfort zone as I have done at The Potter's House Church in Dallas, TX. I don't just go to church, I go to hear the Word that God gives through the man of God and I apply it to my life for change. I always heard him say write the vision down, make it plain. You have to hear it in your spirit before it comes out of your mouth.

From listening and taking it all in, I began a journal writing everything down along the way, and the next thing I knew, God had put in my spirit to write this book to help others to let them know that even though your pain is turned inside out, and no matter what you're facing or going through in all seasons of your life, you can depend on God to see you through.

When you are tried in the fire, you will get the victory. If you stay focused, prayed up and believe that all things are possible to those who love the Lord and are faithful, it shall come to pass in due time in your season. Don't give up. We all need to learn how to balance our lives, but still give service so the blessings will fall upon you and your generations.

I truly thank God for Bishop Jakes and for the spiritual growth I have received in my life under his ministry. This would not be possible, but I kept hearing, don't just read a book write a book. I would have never thought it was possible, but God takes the impossible and make it possible. I'm grateful and humbled, and I thank him for pouring into my spirit every Sunday. May the Lord always give him favor and increase and keep a hedge of protection over him and his family for his faithfulness.

Recognition to Johnny Bogany

I want to thank Minister Johnny Bogany of The Potter's House and of the Acts 2 Ministry where I'm a part of the evangelism team for inspiring me to put the book together and accomplish what he knew I had in me to help, encourage and uplift people who are going through. He motivated me to get started and told me I can do it. He set the tone and directed me in what to do, and I'm so grateful that he believed in me. After reading his book *Finding and Fulfilling Your Purpose Through Dreams and Visions*, I knew I could do it. His book is available on Amazon.

Internal Pain Without Warning In Your Darkest Hour

When unexpected pain comes into your life with death and life threating illness all at one time, what do you do? Who do you talk to? Who would listen and understand the internal pain that feels like a lightning rod burning inside of you. What words can anyone speak into your spirit and understand? Are prayers enough to get you through this unbearable season in your life? Who can speak a word that can wipe the tears away that have left you numb, speechless, and in pain so deep no one can understand unless they have experienced the same or similar to know the helplessness you felt.

The pain turns into anger because you're only human. And you ask yourself, what have I done so bad to have to go through this kind of pain in my life? After the tears, you know you can't stay angry long because you have to put on your weapons of warfare to get you through this horrific season in your life. The only answer is the Word of God no matter how many nights you walked the floor searching for why answers? No matter how many tears you shed even in your sleep. The one thing I can only rely on is the Word of God.

The Bible is true, and it says, He will never leave me nor forsake me. By His stripes I am healed. It says, if two of you shall agree on earth as touching anything that they shall ask for, it shall be done for them by my father which is in heaven. It also says, He will take away all sicknesses and diseases from the midst of us, and He would not put any of the diseases we are afraid of on us.

It says, He will turn the curse into a blessing unto us, be-cause He loves us. Christ has redeemed you from every sickness and every plague. As your days, so shall your strength be. I have healed you and brought up your soul from the grave. I have kept you alive from going down into the pit. I will preserve you and keep you alive.

Sickness is a satanic bondage and you are loosed today. If you need a physician, I am the Lord, your physician. I give you power and authority over all unclean spirits to cast them out, and to heal all manner of sicknesses and diseases. I bore your sickness and I carried your pain. I was put to death for you. I will heal you. I am the Bread of Life. I give you life. Seek me and you shall live. I took your infirmities. If you can believe, all things are possible to those that believe. You shall be buried in good old age.

References:
Hebrews 13:5; Isaiah 53:4-5, 10, 57:19; Matthew 9:12, 10:1, 18:19; Exodus 15:23, 25, 26; Deuteronomy 7:15, 23:5, 28-61, 33:25; Nehemiah 13:2; Galatians 3:13; Psalm 30:1-4, 41:2; Luke 9:1, 13:16, II Corinthians 6:2; John 6:33, Amos 5:4, 6; Matthew 8:17; Mark 9:23, 11:23-24; Genesis 15:15

These scriptures have been my daily food. The pain I have experienced in my life has been overwhelming to a high degree. In July 2017 planning for my family reunion, a perfectly happy day another shock came. My baby brother,

Charles, was so happy to get back to the east coast in New Jersey. He was looking forward to going to the Poconos, Pennsylvania for our family reunion. A beautiful day, him running back and forth to the store happier than ever, especially weeks before enjoying the Manpower Conference at Mega-Fest in Dallas, Texas. I was so excited about how happy he was to get to a session praying and praising the Lord with the men.

I remember my daughter, my mom and my friends enjoying Mega-Fest so much that we all went out to dinner still on a high talking about how great and happy we were at Mega-Fest. Weeks later, my brother never woke up. After shopping all day, he died in his sleep. His heart just stopped. Unfortunately, my mom who house he loved so much to be at, he died at her home.

She tried to bring him back to life, but it was to no avail. He had no heartbeat. What a tragic moment. I spoke earlier about my mother losing her 4th child in 2017, and now, I had to add my 4th sibling to my book in memory of my baby brother, *Pain turned inside out*. What do you do when the unexpected happens and leaves you lost for words? How do you tell his children, especially his 22-year-old son, who was about to get married in a few months, your dad won't be standing with you? What do you do and how do you tell a three-year-old grandson, Pa-Pa is not coming back?

While trying to recover from this tragic ending, I decided that the family reunion should go on, and we should attend. But no sooner than we came to grip with this, my mother was admitted in the hospital. I thought to myself, "Lord, I can't take anymore." What do you do when it is one thing after another and it seems to be no end to your pain?

But right after this, my daughter's dog Deja went blind from diabetes. "I can't believe this. Now, the dog, too?" What do you do in these situations? I kept praying for peace. Yet, another tragedy "hit". And this one really "knocked the life out of me." I became numb and my breathing was sporadic and fast. The report was my only child/daughter was diagnosed with triple negative breast cancer in the same month as we were coming back from family reunion. I thought I cried all the tears I had inside of me from so much pain, but this hit me so hard that I cried for days, weeks, and every time I thought of my daughter more tears streamed down my face. Trying to hide it from my daughter sometimes, I had to walk away so she didn't see the pain that she was feeling herself. After surgery and chemo treatment, which was hard for us (so much side-affects), I thought all these years of money being invested in cancer research why are so many women still being diagnosed with breast cancer. Why?

Why? The ages are getting younger and younger and not enough is being done to help Triple negative cases, and there are not many choices of medicine. Plus, what is not being told about getting a mammogram, unless the doctor sees a reason to order one of concern. Then you have to hope the insurance company pays for it because if you are under 40 years old, insurance companies do not pay for mammograms. Yet, people pay into insurance premiums plans all the time; yet, something that is cited as being a preventable procedure is not covered. People's lives are at stake. This is ridiculous.

What if it was your wife, daughter, niece or aunt? My daughter's life matters, and any other breast cancer patient life matters. Laws need to be changed. It should not matter that it is a small percentage? There are thousands of young women in their 20's and 30's that are dying because insurance companies don't value their lives to invest in them to allow them to have mammograms earlier. It's about early detection. It is about diagnosing these cases early, so lives can be saved. This must stop, and we need more people to speak out before cancer creep into families and they find themselves searching for help.

We are still fighting and praying continually for my daughter, but we need your help to send a message to all the organizations that are giving money to research companies for a cure. We need them to include triple negative breast cancer patients and cancer that spreads throughout the body from breast cancer in their research. More lives would be saved finding a cure to stop this.

Triple negative breast cancer patients have a high recurrence and mortality rate, and these young women are being over looked by researchers because they are a small percentage as a whole, so there is not a whole lot of choices of medicines to give them. But many young women are losing their lives under the age of 40. Breast cancer age has become younger and younger from 20's and 30's, and some in their teens. The young matters and they want to survive also; given a chance at life.

In addition, contact your government, congress, state officials; whomever is making laws on women's health care. Voting matters for change in our health system. Reach out to organizations who you donate money to and find out what research are the monies going to. There are different kinds of breast cancer and all should be equally researched for cures. I pray that the millions of dollars given to these research companies find a better way to help women deal with the side-affects and damages done to their bodies due to breast cancer. Mutilation, one breast or two chopped off leaving them without nipples & dealing with depression and some with low self-esteem, heart damage, neuropathy, bone pain, hair loss, ringing of the ear, sterile in most cases and going into menopause from chemo.

Now if they survive; they have to tell their parents no grandkids/husbands in most cases unless they harvest their eggs, and the majority under 40 with cancer doesn't get a chance because it cost too much and take up too much time before chemo starts. There isn't any financial help to harvest their eggs at this time, but through one company, Livestrong, this organization helps cancer patients by picking up partial pharmaceutical portion for the procedure. However, the person still must come up with $2500 or more; less depending on income at the time. It is shameful not to be able to become pregnant in most cases after chemo.

Mothers who have daughters under 40, and husbands who have wives must voice opinions to everyone who will listen for love ones to be able to have a mammogram under age of 40, and a permanent cure. Insurance companies needs to lower the age to the 20's and 30's. After all you're paying for medical insurance in most cases. They now have 3d images to see dense breast tissues and a better view. Insurance pays if doctors detect a reason. Our daughters, mothers, wives, aunts, nieces, shouldn't have to need a reason if they're under 40 because of the national age for mammograms. It's time for change and getting to the core to stop breast cancer. Lives matter; we have to do more. We are marching and donating money, but how many ask what cancer research is being done for what type of breast cancer? We only hear research, research, that's good, but we need more answers then chemo.

"We are walking on bricks everyday" praying and hoping for a cure, while depending on God. Something has to be done because triple negative "hits" mostly blacks and minority 15% of the entire breast cancer population.

In my research during my daughter's ordeal, there was truly little assistance in any capacity. I asked and surveyed people who know people that had breast cancer or survived breast cancer, and most did not have any assistance financially, especially in the Black community. Sadly to say, we have to do better taking care of our people in this country. However, I want to thank Cancer Care for their donation. I appreciate them as a small organization being filled with compassion to help in some small way. It was greatly appreciated more than you know.

May change come to invest in not just a cure, but the reason why so many women are diagnosed with breast cancer. Let's get to deep answers of why, not just treat the symptoms. Also, let's integrate natural medicines (food with traditional medicines) for a better outlook. Find ways to integrate nutrition with vitamins and healthier organic foods with traditional medicine and exercise for a better outcome.

We are still fighting and praying continually for my daughter, but we need your help. To help stamp out triple negative breast cancer, we need you to definitely call your congress, senator, and government. Don't forget to contact your State officials as well to ask them to fight to pass a law that will include mammograms for women under 40. In addition, I pray that millions of dollars that are given for research for a cure that it would be used to find a better way to offset side-affects often associated with treatments for cancer patients.

We can tell the weather (predict storms, hurricanes, tornadoes, etc.) throughout the world, but we can't get to the core of how to heal cancer overall. Something is truly wrong with this. America have too many intelligent scientists, researchers, and biologists for no cure to exist now for everyone diagnosed with cancer!

I thank everyone that has been on this journey with me through this book, and I thank everyone who's been praying for my daughter. I know that God has a plan for her and her son. I know He didn't take her through this journey of pain to leave her son motherless.

Please continue to pray for her, and her courage and strength. I know God has a plan for each and every one of you. Whatever your fight is never give up or give in. Lastly, if you want to make a donation toward this cause, please go to our GoFundMe pages and give. HELP SALYNDRIA BEAT CANCER. Any amount is acceptable. Please help others with a GoFundMe page. Please don't let them think no one cares. By giving a donation, you are helping these young women who are battling cancer and trying to continue to stay as healthy as they can by what they intake in their bodies. I pray organizations would "step up" and help these young ladies with nutritional guidance, exercise equipment and medical expenses to those who are in need. May they have a compassionate heart. So many women are going through this by themselves. Please reach out to them. Most of them have GoFundMe pages set up and sites. And some of them may need to get re-established in the work field without any backlash. Remember, a lot of them have children and they are praying that they get a second chance to raise their kids and be with their love ones to contribute to society. It is their desire to help someone else when they succeed and survive, to help others who felt lost and uncertain about their future. Pray for them but help them also.

At first, when we needed assistance, my pride would not let me seek help. But the GoFundMe pages are what many people are familiar with and accustomed to giving into. So don't let your pride get in the way of your family getting the help and assistance needed to get through an already difficult time. I'm so thankful for Tetima who set up the GoFundMe page, being persistence with a caring heart along with Reema to do it. I am so blessed for her best friend, Elaine, who journeyed from another state to be by her side during a difficult time during her hospitalization and after surgery. I am also grateful for Heather who blessed my family/Sal during her hospitalization and afterwards. It was greatly appreciated. Thank you all for giving of yourselves with love, who blessed her in anyway. Your love and support will always be appreciated.

Conclusion

Going through all that I endured with my family has been hard for me. But regardless, God has used it and caused me to grow and depend even more on Him. So I want others to know, no matter what they are faced or facing in life never turn your back on God. He will never leave you or forsake you. He is there in your darkest moments and sleepless nights. He is there in your pain. He sees it all.

He is there when tears roll down your face while you are trying to stay strong in sickness, the loss of love ones, unemployment and struggling, and stressed out trying to manage your children without help or support. He is still there.

While writing this book, in pain, I knew God never deserted me in the past and He would not now. He was with me when I shed tears every single day and night while my child and grandson laid in the hospital for three weeks fighting for healing. I cried out to God even though my pain was turned inside out. I cried, "Oh, Lord, help me, I'm only human."

I knew from experiences in the past of being in the valley of the unknown, I could not stop praying and seeking sincere Christians who will come in agreement with me on one accord for my prayers to be more powerful for God to answer them. I take God's promises very seriously. It is amazing that when you are blinded by unexpected circumstances, sicknesses, life threatening illnesses, or emergencies in your life is when God brings you out to do His will.

His will is always to help others, when you come out, so people will know they can survive the storms and valleys they are going through, too. As I watched my mother raising all of her children and suffering in the midst of being the best mom she could be, it taught me to be stronger and how to stand on my own.

I pray that this book has inspired and encouraged you in a positive way for you not to give up on yourself, regardless of the circumstances or situations you are facing now or in the future. But if you are growing weary, let me encourage you to take a deep breath and get back into the race. Don't wait on others to encourage you, just encourage yourself.

You are not alone even if it seems that way. Even if people leave you or betrayed you, you are still not alone. Not even for a moment. God is with you day and night just call on Him. He will cancel fear and any other stressors of life (anger, frustration, doubt, etc.) from out of your spirit and mind if you just depend on Him.

In these moments, don't depend on your own strength. Your own strength will always be inadequate. You cannot do anything on your own strength, especially if you are lost mentally, emotionally, and spiritually. We need God in our lives to turn things around. I never could have survived all that I have been through and what I have witness without God. Loosing so many people to death in my life and watching my mom grieve over the loss of four children, and I, myself, grieve over the same loss (losing four siblings), and dealing with a daughter surviving cancer in 2017. We still need prayer, but I'm trusting God still.

We need God and you do, too. Whatever your pain is may you take the time to get saved if it's in your spirit to do so by the salvation prayer in this book. I pray for God's presence to be in your life. I pray you get to know God for yourself and know His voice. I pray your prayers are answered as miracles take place. I pray you experience a new beginning with great things happening. I pray for your healing and that a revival takes place in your homes and that your dreams and visions are fulfilled. I pray that sickness is cancelled out of your life and that the promises of God will be manifested in your life for many years to come. The Word of God says, my sheep knows my voice. I pray that you hear and obey the voice of God, so you can be connected to a Bible teaching church to grow in your faith more. May this bless you and you be a blessing to others.

PRAYERS

Prayer For Healing And Restoration

Father, I come to You with faith for Your people knowing that so many are going through and have so many obstacles in their lives. If it's not this, then it's that. Father, sometimes misfortunate things happen through no fault of their own, because the enemy comes to steal and kill, trying to destroy what You already have spoken over them.

Father, sometimes the struggles in their daily lives can be so unbearable that they need a touch from You or it won't work. So many of Your people are walking with disbelief because they are suffering so much and can't find relief. Even when things seem as if it isn't getting any better, and the pain is too strong to speak to another for help because they feel they won't understand what they are going through. Father, please speak to Your people right where they are. They need your Word to radiate down in their spirit with a confirmation that You hadn't forgotten about them. So whatever they are facing or going through that they shall have victory; they shall see the light again. They need to know that their load will get lighter. Their love ones or themselves will be healed, and that they will get the help they need through the right Christian doctors, and the right hospital. Father, connect them with the right people in their lives, so they will know You sent help and to walk with them as You walk beside them in the storm of darkness.

Mark 11:22-24: Have faith in God. For surely, I say unto you, whatsoever you say to this mountain, be removed and be cast into the sea, and do not doubt (waiver) in his heart, but believe that those things he said will be done. He will have whatever he says. Therefore, I say to you whatever things you ask for when you pray, believe that you receive them, and you shall have them.

Whose report will you believe? Romans 10:17 says, "Faith comes by hearing, and hearing comes by the Word of God." We must listen to that still small voice in our spirit trusting that God hears, understands, and will bring us out in His timing whatever we are going through. It is just for a season, the thing we are enduring, even though sometimes it seems like a lifetime when you are in it. God is still in the midst of it all, and He will not let you fall among your enemies. He got you. Be strong in the Word no matter what you are going through.

Father, I ask for healing and restoration in all areas of their lives. May they be better than they were in all areas. Let them never be the same again. May a new normal fall upon them. May the crooked places turn straight in their lives. Father, You said knock, and they are knocking. You said ask, and they are petitioning their prayers to You crying out for mercy and grace. Praying that You see their circumstances and come to their rescue. I pray that they will receive speedy answers to the nightmare of unbelief of what they are going through and facing. Give them the peace that surpasses all understanding. Clothes them with love in their hearts and spirits. Equip them with compassion and humility so they may know your unconditional love. I give you the honor and the glory that it's already done. I pray that the people who read this prayer and need You will be filled with your spirit and their life will never be the same, and the doors that has been closed will began to open up for victory in their lives. Whatever lies that have been spoken over them may it be canceled in Christ Jesus' name, Amen!

It was in my heart and spirit just to pray for people who had been going through difficult times in life. As you have read, I have had to deal with a lot in the areas of sickness, pain, and struggles, and I am not sure why, especially when I know I am a good person and always try to up-lift and help others. But sometimes life just throw you an anchor to keep you falling downwards. But know in these seasons, you have to pick yourself up and get back in the race knowing that these seasons are not forever. Just trust God and He will walk you through your valley -- whatever you are going through. I want you to know someone cares about you enough to want to pray for you to let you know don't give up on yourself or family. God loves you and He will order your steps; He is walking with you. Just call on Him and reach back for that mustard seed of faith and stretch it until the miracle comes -- until you receive your victory in Christ Jesus. God bless!

Prayer of Victory

Father, please touch me and everyone in my household. Touch the sick, heal them from the top of their head to the bottom of their feet. Touch every organ, muscle, heart, lung, bone, vein, eye, female organ, male organ, and any other part of their body. Father, cancel out generational sicknesses and diseases in my family as we cry out to You. Cancel out stress, anger, suicide, frustration, offensive behavior, lying spirit, and dysfunctional household. Heal marriages, families, children, fathers; cancel out depression, cancel out loneliness, sadness, and argumentative spirits. Father, You said, if two of us come together on earth touching and agreeing on anything, it shall be done of the Father which is in heaven. Today, I pray for all generational curses to be broken in all my families. I pray for a sweet spirit. I pray for my generations and families to receive this word for their lives. I pray for a re-dedication of my family to be uplifted, encouraged, and to have renewed minds. May they all receive a new way of thinking; new perspective of how we view our households, our spouses, our children and family members. I thank You because You are the Alpha and Omega; all knowing One. I lift these prayers up to You for change and for canceling out all generational curses across the land. Amen!

Prayer Against Depression

Lord, I pray for every hurting soul. I pray that depression leaves their minds, spirits, and souls. I pray for a renewed mind. I pray that the prayer of faith shall heal them and that God shall raise them back up and if any committed sin, it shall be forgiven (James 5:15).

I cancel the assignment of the enemy over their minds. I pray that they be healed and made whole. I pray that whatever got them into this state of mind that it be canceled totally. I pray that Satan have no rights, no power over Your people. I pray that light shine upon them. I pray laughter returns to their spirits. I pray that strongholds be broken over their minds, in their lives, in their homes, in their families, in their marriages, in their children, on their jobs, in their relationships, and whomever is connected to them.

I pray that You release the right people into their lives so mistakes won't be repeated to keep taking them downhill. I pray that You connect them with the right relationships in their lives. I pray for new beginnings. I pray for families to reunite. I pray for the men to come to their senses and to see the gifts God gave them when they find a good woman for a wife. I pray for communications in the homes with their families and in their relationships. I pray the devil out of their homes. I pray demonic attacks have no more power on God's people -- those who believe that He is King of Kings. I pray that anger leaves the minds of Your hurting people and replace it with love. I pray that love overcomes the peo-

ple so they will know how to respect one another. I pray that judgmental spirits are canceled out of all relationships.

I pray supernaturally that prayer returns to every school in America so our children will be free from bondage in their minds and freed from adversity and bullying. I pray the little ones will grow up with the Word of God embedded in their spirits. They will pray at a young age with their parents, with their siblings, and in the church with one another.

Prayer is power. We have to learn to thank God for taking us to the next level with high expectations and blessings with a renewed mind. The only way is to pass the test of hearing from God and be led by His Word by going through the process without complaining; just know He will never leave you alone if you take the Word of God with you.

Father, I thank You for healing Your people. I sincerely pray that everyone is uplifted and encouraged today to know God is still with them through their valleys of darkness and that You will bring them through stronger and wiser with a renewed mind thinking differently than before. May joy cometh in the morning. May their tears and sadness turn into victory. I pray for answered prayers. God bless you.

Lord, I pray for the people who has been praying for the fruit of love. Lord, open their eyes so they can see the natural unconditional love that comes from You. Let them see the mighty fruit of Your love for the hurting and the lonely. And *the ones that gave so much of themselves, the ones that think the fruit of love and unity is no longer for them. The devil is a liar, God is still in charge and He knows your heart and knows what you need, just reach out to Him so He can heal you, so you can be fruitful in all areas of your life again. God is love.*

My Prayer For You

He is Jehovah Rapha, King of Kings, Lord of Lords, Alpha and Omega. He can heal when the doctors can't. He can turn your situation around in the midst of the enemy. Father, touch all who are sick.

Touch every organ in their bodies. Father, cancel out breast cancer, prostate cancer. Touch every soul that's dealing with some kind of cancer and destroy the cells with the infirmities. Put a hedge of protection around your children dealing with sickness and diseases. I pray that the cells of cancer dry up like dead bones and never to return again in your people bodies -- have Your way, heal all people of every kind of sickness and disease.

Touch every heart and lung in their bodies and reverse the curse. Reverse their situations. I plead the blood over every- one that receives this prayer in their spirit. May God make you whole and healthy, and give you another chance. And Father protect pregnant women everywhere. Cover them and their child, protect their unborn and deliver them into the world safely. Heal the mothers' bodies; heal their minds. I cancel stress and postpartum depression.

Satan take your hands off of God's people. God, I ask you to reverse stroke and heart attacks, catch it before it occurs. And people who have had it, put a hedge of protection around their hearts, brains and bodies. Make them stronger every step. May no damages occur that will set them back. Fa-

ther, touch all the women out there who desire to be a mother. Give them the gift of life of motherhood and protect them as they walk with You in the newness of Your miracles. Put Satan to shame; You have the power even in life.

I thank You for Your glory and grace and praise -- Your name for all that You have done for everyone, and all that You're going to do to show who's in charge. Protect all, especially people with high blood pressure and diabetes. Protect their arteries, sight and limbs in the Almighty Christ Jesus' name. Amen!

Prayer of Expectations

Sometimes we just have to believe by faith that all things are possible to those who truly walk by faith. We must pray and speak it out into the atmosphere. Words have power, speak it out loud and believe it by faith. Say this:

I expect to be healed. I am healed. I expect my heart to work right. I expect my blood pressure to be lowered. I expect God to have His hands on my life. I expect by faith for more air to pour into my lungs. I expect by faith, and decree and declare my body to be free of sickness and disease. I lift it all up to God, for He know the thoughts He thinks towards me, thoughts of peace and not evil for an expected end. I expect victory according to Jeremiah 29:11.

God knows what you are going through, and He got you. Get a prayer partner and someone you can trust and pray together. Pray with your spouse, your children, and family. You can change the family with one word from the Lord. He gives grace and mercy every day, even when we don't deserve it, Have mercy on us all, Lord!

Prayer of Salvation

I pray for a cancellation of low self-esteem, frustration, anger, lack of love or no love, negativity, liars, betrayals, cheaters, sex addicts, and all kind of craziness. I pray God will do a new thing in your life, and He will give you a new perspective of how you see life as a whole. I pray the enemy is "stop in his tracks." I pray for healing of the spirit and minds. I pray for your emotions to calm down and for you to know you are not alone. That you would know He is carrying you. I pray for marriages, relationships, families, and broken homes. I pray for the men to be re-established in the homes -- first in their minds and then in their spirits. I pray that everyone who's been through or going through, and don't know who to call on, will call on God, the Savior, Jesus Christ, who died for us so we can have life abundantly. I pray for a new you, and that you give your life to Christ. I pray these words penetrate your spirit, mind and heart to produce change.

If you want change, a new way of doing things, and you want to be focused on new dreams, visions and God's purpose for your life, then repeat these words using your name.

I (Your Name) repent of all my sins — past and present. I believe that Christ was born, and He is the Son of God. He died on the cross for me. I believe in my heart, and I confess with my mouth that Christ was born. He died on the cross for me. I confess with my mouth that Christ was raised from the dead and is now seated at the right hand of the Father.

Romans 10:9:

That thou shalt confess with thy mouth the Lord Jesus Christ, and shalt believe in thine heart that God hath raise him from the dead, thou shalt be saved. For with the heart man believeth unto righteousness; and with the mouth confession is made unto salvation.

Please get a Bible and read it. Meditate on the scriptures pertaining to your situation and circumstances. Pray about God's will for your life. Find a Bible believing church with an anointed pastor that teaches the Word of God. Get involved with the different ministries of what the church has to offer; find the ones that fit your needs for growth to help keep you strong in your faith.

www.ingramcontent.com/pod-product-compliance
Lightning Source LLC
Chambersburg PA
CBHW050634150426

42811CB00052B/808